SUBORDINATING
THE POOR

Joe R. Feagin is on a sabbatical from the University of Texas, Austin, while he works with the United States Commission on Civil Rights. He is the author of numerous articles and books dealing with the poor and race relations in America, including *Ghetto Revolts* (with Harlan Hahn) and *The Urban Scene*.

SUBORDINATING THE POOR

Welfare and American Beliefs

JOE R. FEAGIN

Prentice-Hall, Inc. Englewood Cliffs, New Jersey
A SPECTRUM BOOK

Library of Congress Cataloging in Publication Data

FEAGIN, JOE R
    Subordinating the poor.

    (A Spectrum Book)
    Includes bibliographical references.
        1. Public welfare—United States.   2. Poor—
    United States.   3. Public welfare—United States—
    Public Opinion.   4. Poor—United States—Public
    opinion.   5. Public opinion—United States.   I. Title.
    HV91.F38   362.5'0973   75-4941
    ISBN 0-13-859140-7
    ISBN 0-13-859132-6 pbk.

10   9   8   7   6   5   4   3

PRENTICE-HALL INTERNATIONAL, INC. *(London)*
PRENTICE-HALL OF AUSTRALIA PTY. LTD. *(Sydney)*
PRENTICE-HALL OF CANADA LTD. *(Toronto)*
PRENTICE-HALL OF INDIA PRIVATE LIMITED *(New Delhi)*
PRENTICE-HALL OF JAPAN, INC. *(Tokyo)*
PRENTICE-HALL OF SOUTHEAST ASIA (PTE.) LTD. *(Singapore)*

Contents

Preface

As this book goes to press, issues of poverty and welfare generally remain in the background in public policy discussions, while the issues of energy, the depressed state of the economy, and world diplomacy take precedence. Yet poverty and welfare matters doubtless will reappear in public policy discussions in the near future, catapulted there by economic events. Indeed, recent stories in the press have stressed the continuing problems of health care and hunger among poor Americans in the mid-1970s. Modest (but temporary?) public employment programs have been implemented to cope with the growing number of the unemployed. Trial balloons have been floated in Washington, D.C. indicating a new interest in reviving proposals similar to ex-President Richard M. Nixon's ill-fated welfare reform proposal (Family Assistance Plan). Such government action could lead to a further federalization of the American welfare system.

Whatever future changes occur in the welfare system—and undoubtedly there will be some important changes—books such as this provide some social and historical context helpful in making sense out of past, present, and future public attempts to deal with the poor. This collection of exploratory essays is directed toward that end.

If one purpose of writing books is to further one's own learning process, that has been accomplished here. This writing has led me to consider numerous new questions about poverty and welfare. While some of these have been tentatively resolved here, others are just beginning to shape my future research. A number of able colleagues have read various portions of this manuscript and have contributed significantly to this learning process. I am particularly grateful to David Perry, David Austin, Jorge Bustamante, Raymond Mohl, and Louis Schneider for their critical review of various draft chapters of this manuscript. I am also indebted to N.I.M.H. for a research grant that enabled me to conduct the survey discussed in Chapters 4 and 5 and to Joseph Goeke and his associates at the Opinion Research Corporation (Princeton, New Jersey) for helping to expedite that survey. Patsy Taylor and Robert Perrin provided research assistance in coding and analyzing the survey data, and I am grateful for their help. As always, I owe more than I can recount here to my wife Clairece, who assisted as typist, discussant, and friend while this book was being written.

SUBORDINATING
THE POOR

1
Introduction

Concern with poverty and welfare aid for the very poor has been a roller coaster phenomenon over the last few centuries of Western history, rising and falling with such things as changes in economic conditions, in political protest, and the character of political leadership. This oscillation has characterized not only the governing elites but the public as well; in the three centuries of American development, both public interest and government action in the area of relief for the poor have fluctuated significantly. Not that poverty and welfare have ever been neutral issues for most Americans—indeed, few topics have generated more mixed feelings or even hostility. Yet it is only periodically that public attention and discussion have focused so intensely on these issues that concrete action has become a top government priority.

In this country in the 1930s a major depression and consequent political upheaval forced new government action on behalf of the destitute, which resulted in the development of relief programs including those federally subsidized public assistance programs now commonly termed "welfare." In the 1940s and 1950s there seemed to be a relative decrease in government and popular concern with the poor, perhaps the result of an emerging confidence that the "affluent society" had arrived. Particularly in the 1950s, both scholars and government officials emphasized the new wave of prosperity in the United States. In the view of many, poverty was all but vanquished and most citizens would soon be affluent suburbanites. In 1958, John Kenneth Galbraith heralded this new age in an important book, *The Affluent Society*. Arguing that the United States had achieved the status of an affluent society and was thus in need of new economic guidance, he suggested that poverty survived in economic discussions primarily because it supported conventional wisdom—that it could no longer be seen as a major affliction in the United States, but as "an afterthought." [1] This theme was common among members of the economic and political elites. As a result, these were years in which aid for the poor received only modest government attention.

Lack of interest in poverty in the 1950s was replaced by a rediscovery of poverty in the 1960s. But defenders of welfare or of welfare recipients were not easy to find as concern with the persistence of welfare and its rising costs became an issue in the public speeches and comments of many leaders. Conservative and moderate leaders discussed the subject widely and vigorously; as for liberal leaders, it seemed that they often preferred to duck the problem altogether. Countless words and much advice flowed from governors, city government officials, presidents, business officials, editors, and concerned citizens. In elections incumbents were always fair game on the welfare issue. Business leaders reiterated themes linked to the "welfare crisis." Periodicals such as *Life* and *Reader's Digest* began to focus on the "welfare mess," and editors of newspapers in communities of varying size periodically criticized existing welfare programs.

Over the last decade or so moderate and conservative leaders have continued to be the most likely to articulate publicly their critical views of welfare programs and recipients, and to suggest work-oriented cures for welfare ills. Though many of these commentators expressed some concern for the plight of the poor, it often seemed mechanical, with the real meat of the message delivered in a manner explicitly or implicitly evoking a stereotyped image of the poor that emphasized their lack of effort, their low ambitions, or their need for stimulus to work rather than such important issues as low relief payments or the lack of jobs indicated by high unemployment rates. This image of the poor has been perpetuated in much discussion of the welfare problem in recent decades.

SOME PUBLIC COMMENTS

In the early 1960s Joseph Mitchell, then the city manager of Newburgh, New York, inaugurated a hard-hitting campaign designed to reduce the number of poor on the Newburgh welfare rolls by strict new regulations, at least one of which was subsequently declared to be illegal. In an important speech Mitchell indicated his views of welfare recipients, as well as the goals of the Newburgh "reforms":

We challenged the right of social parasites to breed illegitimate children at the taxpayer's expense. We challenged the right of moral chiselers and loafers to squat on the relief rolls forever. We challenged the right of cheaters to make more on relief than when working. We challenged the right of those on relief to loaf by State and Federal edict. We challenged the right of people to quit jobs at will and go on relief like spoiled children. We challenged the right of citizens to migrate for the purpose of becoming or continuing as public charges.[2]

Newburgh quickly became a symbol of a city taking concrete action to deal with the undeserving poor. Newspapers in many cities ran editorials in favor of restrictive welfare actions, and national magazines published critiques of welfare drawing on these conventional images. Although some criticism of Mitchell's views and Newburgh's actions did come from liberal journals and welfare professionals, and even though the Newburgh reforms were eventually rescinded, the millions of words published on the subject reinforced the negative picture of the poor among both average citizens and members of the governing elite.[3]

Some national figures supported Newburgh's restrictive welfare actions. For example, Senator Barry Goldwater wrote a letter to the city manager saying, in part, that the "abuses in the welfare field are mounting and the only way to curtail them are the steps which you have already taken."[4] Many other leaders agreed that such restrictive "reforms" would be good for all cities. The effect on citizens was one of crystallizing attitudes and catapulting welfare into major political prominence; Newburgh had become the stimulus for discussing welfare issues among leaders and citizens throughout the country.

In his subsequent campaign for the presidential nomination and for the presidency, Senator Goldwater made welfare and related poverty programs an issue. In a New York speech he conjured up the image of the poor who lack ambition: "The fact is that most people who have no skill, have had no education for the same reason—low intelligence or low ambition." [5] In his view the solution lay in a forced-work program; he argued that "those who are physically able to work should be put to work to earn their benefits at a specified rate per hour." Apparently, a low wage rate would suffice. The image of large numbers of lazy but able-bodied welfare recipients implicit in these views, as well as the suggestion of a forced-work solution, probably reflected, and shaped, the views of millions of Americans.

In these early years of the 1960s a few major national political figures took some action to deal with welfare and poverty problems. President John F. Kennedy generated programs directed toward services and work-oriented counseling for the welfare poor. In his message to Congress on the 1962 social service amendments, Kennedy underlined the importance of non-economic factors in the problems of the welfare poor and called for more than a "relief check"; he stressed the need for "positive services and solutions . . . to help our less fortunate citizens help themselves." [6] President Lyndon B. Johnson accented a somewhat similar approach in his famous War on Poverty; but although he seldom publicly commented on welfare or the welfare poor, he did on occasion seem critical of welfare. In his speeches and messages on poverty he sometimes emphasized this contrast: "We are not trying to give people more relief—we want to give people more opportunity." [7] As Valentine has pointed out, in practice this War-on-Poverty approach tended to reinforce the traditional welfare orientation, utilizing as it did a negative image of the poor and their subculture.[8] The subculture of poverty was often seen as pathological, disorganized, and contradictory to middle-class values emphasizing hard work, motivation to strive, thrift, and stable family life. The solution to this pathology was to change the culture and values of the poor by means of expanded social work, education, psychiatry, and training programs. In contrast to conservative sentiment, the orientation was to greater federal government involvement aimed at both relieving the suffering of the poor and reforming their morals, values, and attitudes. "The basic message of this approach to the poor is that only after they have become conventionally respectable can they hope for a chance to leave poverty behind them."[9]

Prominent state leaders also commented on welfare issues in the 1960s. For example, in a major 1966 telecast Ronald Reagan, who would soon be governor of the nation's largest state, also played up the image of undeserving masses of recipients. He argued for a firm state policy on work requirements: "From now on the able-bodied will work for their keep or take job training to fit themselves for jobs, and there'll be no pay for play."[10] In his campaign he criticized welfare programs and the "welfare state," a phrase which seemed to include federal involvement in many areas. In his first inaugural address as governor he proposed a "no-nonsense" approach to public welfare in California:

But we are not going to perpetuate poverty by substituting a permanent dole for a paycheck. There is no humanity or charity in destroying self-reliance, dignity and self-respect . . . the very substance of moral fiber.[11]

In this address Reagan did say in passing that he supported aid for the truly needy, such as the disabled and the aged, but—as was true of many leaders who commented on welfare in that decade—he did not give much attention to their economic plight or deal with the flaws in the surrounding social and economic system, such as racial discrimination or high rates of unemployment, which might be relevant to the welfare situation in general. The conventional critique of welfare and welfare recipients, in fact, has been suggested as much by what is *not* mentioned as by what is said.

Indeed, this often seemed to be the case in the speeches and public messages of the first president to become actively and prominently involved in major proposals for welfare reform, Richard M. Nixon. Even while he was proposing modest innovations to reshape existing welfare programs, Nixon's comments on welfare sometimes implied that he too held the familiar stereotyped view of the welfare recipient. In his 1969 welfare reform message to Congress he argued that the present welfare system was a failure, that it had "even deepened dependency by all too often making it more attractive to go on welfare than to go to work." [12] Here again is the image of the recipient who prefers welfare to a reasonable job. To prevent the "shiftless poor" from taking advantage of his welfare reform program he frequently underlined the need for a work requirement:

Thus, they must accept training opportunities and jobs when offered, or give up their right to the new payments for themselves. No able-bodied person will have a "free ride" in a nation that provides opportunity for training and work.[13]

Later, in his acceptance speech at the 1972 Republican convention, Nixon again reinforced the negative cast of his beliefs:

I say that instead of providing incentives for millions of more Americans to go on welfare, we need a program which will provide incentives for people to get off welfare and get to work.[14]

However, it must be pointed out that Nixon did express concern for the economic difficulties of disabled, aged, and mothers with small children. Perhaps of all those leaders greatly influential in the public discussion of welfare in the 1960s and early 1970s he, probably because of the influence of certain advisers, gave more attention to innovative reform. He was the first president to press for a modest family assistance plan, although this proposal was later abandoned. This plan would in effect have provided a guaranteed (but very low) minimum income for most poor families, including families on welfare. Nonetheless, Nixon still spoke of welfare programs and recipients in terms of a work ethic language that doubtless reinforced the familiar stereotypes many people held of the welfare poor.

During this period, Senator Russell B. Long also made a number of important comments and speeches on welfare programs and recipients. Suggestive of the prevailing image was the following:

In my opinion, a solution to the problem of family desertion and illegitimacy will do more to correct the welfare mess than any other action we can take. Paternity and support suits enforced by the Federal Government can create a semblance of responsibility and discipline in an area where irresponsibility and permissiveness have too long prevailed.[15]

Later, he made some additional statements on the welfare types who, he emphasized, were a major part of the problem:

I am no newcomer to the welfare scene. My record on behalf of the poor is clear. But I am concerned—gravely concerned—that the welfare system, as we know it today, is being manipulated and abused by malingerers, cheats and outright frauds to the detriment not only of the American taxpayers whose dollars support the program, but also to the detriment of the truly needy on whose behalf the Federal-State system of cash assistance is so important.

There is no question in anyone's mind that the present welfare system is a mess.[16]

Although Long also mentions the "truly needy" in this speech, they seem to be a secondary consideration compared to the need to get immoral recipients off the rolls.

Of course, government leaders have not been the only influential people publicly debating welfare in the last decade. From time to time other leaders such as business officials and newspaper editors have also taken a pessimistic view of the "welfare crisis." For example, one strong comment came from a nationally syndicated editor of the *Tulsa Tribune* in a speech before a press association:

Relief is gradually becoming an honorable career in America. It is a pretty fair life, if you have neither conscience nor pride. The politicians will weep over you. The state will give a mother a bonus for her illegitimate children, and if she neglects them sufficiently she can save enough of her ADC payments to keep herself and her boyfriend in wine and gin. Nothing is your fault.[17]

Here again in a public analysis the stress is on illegitimacy, immorality, and permanent dependency.

Proposals by business leaders for welfare reform often highlighted the need for a work incentive in reshaping public welfare programs. Plans for change have typically been suffused with a strong dose of the work ethic. Thus, late in 1967 the chairman of the board of the Chase Manhattan Bank called for work-oriented welfare reforms, the benefits of which he underlined:

The "incentive" approach to welfare puts great stock in these old-fashioned—but today largely neglected—ideas of individual responsibility, personal character, and the belief that every man is, in fact, his "brother's keeper." [18]

This presumed decline in the ideology of individualism has been a preoccupation of many prominent leaders over the last decade, and we will deal with it in depth in this book.

Looking over these comments by leaders and people of influence, we can see that they frequently expressed mixed feelings about the welfare poor. Sometimes they seemed to distinguish between the "undeserving" poor and the "deserving" poor; at other times this distinction seemed to give way to a one-sided picture of all the poor as ignorant and lazy rejectors of the tenets of the American work ethic.

THE AVERAGE AMERICAN

Over the last decade or two rank-and-file Americans have been questioned regarding their feelings about the poor, including the welfare poor. Their responses have indicated that the plight of the poor is often considered secondary to the assumed shiftlessness and immorality of the poor. Comments by rank-and-file workers, such as the following by a Chicago cab driver, are often more colorful than those made by politicians and business leaders:

About welfare? What do I think about the welfare? It ought to be cut back. The goddamn people sit around when they should be working and then they're having illegitimate kids to get more money. You know, their morals are different. They don't give a damn. Stop it. That's what I say. These people they don't work. They don't pay taxes.[19]

In a study in the late 1950s Robert Lane encountered a related perspective in interviews with "Middle Americans":

But then you get a lot of people who don't want to work; you get welfare. People will go on living on that welfare—they're happier than hell. Why should they work if the city will support them? [20]

This view is close to the "welfare Cadillac" image, the view that those on welfare are happy and living a life of ease. Another "man on the street" quote also blames the lack of a work ethic among the welfare poor:

I don't think they should get any more. I have some opinions on that, and I think that all of the people on relief should be made to work because I think half of them are bums.[21]

This same respondent went on to underline the "boozing it up" pattern assumed to be characteristic of relief recipients.

Coles found a considerable concern among "Middle Americans" for the lazy poor during interviews in the late 1960s. Indeed, the rioting and demonstrating in the sixties were sometimes tied in with the welfare situation; one of Coles' respondents criticizes the poor for political turmoil:

It's the ones on welfare and they're the colored mostly, right? And when people stop trying to pull themselves up, and when instead they take all they can get from the government, and when they get by rioting and stealing and demonstrating and demanding from other people what they can't con the rest of us into giving them—then that's wrong, and I'm against it.[22]

Here is one public image of black welfare recipients and of those who are unwilling to help themselves, yet resort to troublemaking. Another worker, a young welder, spoke of discussions about welfare chiseling among workers in his group:

We argue during coffee break. One guy will say that Nixon is cracking down on the nigger-bums, and the welfare-bleeders, who cheat on the city and the state and loaf at our expense, the taxpayers.[23]

In looking through reported interviews with various "Middle Americans" over the last decade or two, one occasionally finds sympathetic assessments of the lives and conditions faced by poor Americans, but, as with many prominent American leaders, these usually appear secondary to negative viewpoints.

CONCLUSION

Of course, these opinions provide only a small and selective sample of comments which, explicitly or implicitly, suggest the negative attitude toward the welfare poor. Obviously, other public statements were made during the 1960s, a few of which implied more favorable images. Some leaders, including members of Congress, have occasionally defended the poor eloquently. For example, note the words of one prominent Representative:

I find the hypocrisy of those who are now demanding freedom of choice to work or not to work for welfare mothers beyond belief. The truth is these women never have had freedom of choice. They have never been free to work. Their education has been inadequate and the market has been unable to absorb their talents. . . .

Can you imagine any conditions more demoralizing than those welfare mothers live under? [24]

Moreover, a few government commissions during the 1960s, such as the national Advisory Council on Public Welfare, issued reports with a more sympathetic outlook, although their opinions did not receive great publicity.

On the whole, it is difficult to find public comments from this period that are strongly favorable to the welfare poor, particularly from members of influential and powerful elites. Structural problems such as the lack of decent-paying jobs, low welfare payments in many areas, and discrimination were usually not emphatically raised. Critiques of the system surrounding the welfare poor were often missing. Sometimes liberal editors and congressmen criticized unfair regulations or harsh public comments, but few went so far as to publicly praise the heroism and courage of the welfare poor. A major emphasis even among liberals in drafting solutions to welfare problems was on the work ethic. In spite of a few departures from conventional ideas, the negative images seemed to have dominated welfare discussions in the last two decades, and counterattacks against prevailing images were few and ineffective.

Looking at the controversy over welfare and welfare reform, one might well ask why a resurgence of interest in these issues occurred in the decade of the 1960s. A number of factors seem to have been important. One may well have been the publicizing of new statistics in the early 1960s showing that 36 million Americans—about one-fifth of the population—were poor. Statistics on welfare recipients and welfare costs, which were now systematically collected, were also widely cited by the mid- and late 1960s. All government (federal, state, and local) expenditures for cash public assistance—the conventional definition of welfare—increased from $3.2 billion in 1957 to $5.4 billion in 1964. By the end of the decade the 1964 figure had more than doubled. The number of recipients also increased over the 1960s, rising from 6.3 million in 1959 to 10.7 million in 1969. Increases in these figures helped generate publicity and official concern for a "welfare crisis." Other factors also played an important role in generating concern with welfare, but this concern had a different focus. These included minority protest movements, such as the civil rights movement among black Americans. Political protest among the nonwhite poor made it difficult for leaders to assign poverty and welfare issues a low priority. Of importance too was the growth in organization of welfare rights groups, which attempted to publicize the problems of the welfare poor. Political pressures from the poor were ignored by many, but they stimulated others to discuss welfare reform. Yet another factor of considerable importance in the increased public attention to welfare in the 1960s was the rising cost of state and local government. Much of the new attention zeroing in on welfare issues seemed to be motivated by a concern for the general fiscal difficulties of local governments.

A NOTE ON ORGANIZATION

A primary purpose of this book is to explore basic American perspectives on the poor, particularly those who require public aid. To this end we will draw on several types of data, including the details of concrete government actions and public opinion polls. In Chapter 2, the historical background of contemporary welfare patterns and perspectives in the United States will be examined. It is of course difficult to separate public actions from public views, so we will look at government laws and programs for clues to views of the welfare poor. Relief programs usually reflect basic values. In that chapter the ideology of individualism (which has also been called the "Protestant ethic" or the "work ethic") will be discussed, particularly the development of fundamental beliefs in the crucible of Protestantism. Chapter 2 also depicts the way in which the English dealt with the poor in their attitudes and laws, providing important background for the historical development of public aid, first in the American colonies, then in the United States. The contributions of Protestant thought, of social Darwinism, and of the frontier ethic to American individualism are briefly explored, as is the impact of individualism and related beliefs on actual welfare programs. The concluding section of Chapter 2 reviews the emergence of dramatic new actions on behalf of the poor in the 1930s, actions which, under the Social Security Act, laid the groundwork for a federally subsidized public welfare system.

Chapter 3 is an essay on the welfare system which has emerged since the 1930s and attempts to explore both its goals and current structure. The broader context of public aid to the poor is briefly examined, along with the economic subsidies that have gone to *nonpoor* Americans. The welfare goals of relief of suffering, defusing protest, increasing work effort, and reforming the morals of the poor are discussed, followed by an analysis of the implementation of these goals in concrete government actions and programs in the last few decades. The structure of the existing welfare system—its basic subsystems and external determinants—is traced as a framework for looking at the recent history of the welfare system. Issues considered in reviewing that recent history are Congress and welfare, the presidency and welfare, welfare localism, local noncompliance with federal law, recent court decisions, and the secondary labor market. We will also note some recent challenges to the welfare system from the "bottom up," in the form of welfare rights protest movements.

Chapter 4 more completely discusses the ideology of individualism, with a heavy emphasis on its negative side, as an important determinant of the American welfare system. By the "negative" side is meant those beliefs which see economic failure—poverty or dependence on public welfare—as a sign of individual character defects and personal immorality. Drawing on a recent nationwide survey, opinions about the poor, the causes of poverty, welfare, and welfare recipients are explored in some detail. The concluding section of the chapter analyzes the probable functions and consequences of anti-poor and anti-welfare attitudes and suggests that these views, in part, reflect a false consciousness among average Americans—a focusing of misdirected hostility on those below and a separating of workers from one another. The issue of ideological repression of workers is also raised in this chapter.

Chapter 5, the concluding chapter, grapples with a number of alternatives that have been suggested as solutions, partial or total, to the welfare system established in the last few decades and discusses recent proposals in the context of public opinions and viewpoints. The nationwide survey is further analyzed to assess public support for a guaranteed-income plan, a guaranteed-job plan, and a proposal for equalizing family incomes. The persisting strength of the work ethic is again revealed, as is the reluctance of citizens to propose or come to grips with proposals for substantial economic equality. In conclusion, the issue of change in individualistic perspectives is examined, together with the possibilities for major economic reform in a country committed to the ideology of individualism.

Everyday life in the United States has been suffused for more than three centuries with the ideology of individualism. And this ideology, arguments to the contrary notwithstanding, is far from dead in the United States. This set of exploratory essays is not designed as a final or general analysis of individualism—that important task remains yet to be done. Rather, the text represents an attempt to explore work ethic perspectives primarily as they relate to beliefs about and programs for the poor. Our concern therefore will be the impact of the individualistic ethic in those areas in which it manifests itself in government welfare programs, expressed public opinion, and the development of alternatives to welfare.

1. John Kenneth Galbraith, *The Affluent Society* (London: Penguin Books, 1962), p. 260.

2. Speech by Joseph M. Mitchell, *Vital Speeches*, xxviii (December 15, 1961), 215.

3. See Edgar May, *The Wasted Americans* (New York: Signet Books, 1965), pp. 36–45.

4. Quoted in May, p. 37.

5. Speech by Barry Goldwater, *The New York Times*, January 16, 1964, p. 21.

6. Quoted in May, *The Wasted Americans*, p. 187.

7. Quoted in Donald G. Howard, *Social Welfare* (New York: Random House, 1969), p. 108.

8. Charles A. Valentine, *Culture and Poverty* (Chicago: University of Chicago Press, 1968), pp. 144–55.

9. *Ibid.*, p. 145.

10. Speech by Ronald Reagan, *The New York Times*, September 10, 1966, p. 13.

11. Inaugural address by Ronald Reagan, *The New York Times*, January 6, 1967, p. 18.

12. Richard M. Nixon, "Welfare Reform: A Message from the President of the United States," in *Poverty Policy*, ed. Theodore R. Marmor (Chicago: Aldine, 1971), p. 78.

13. *Ibid.*, p. 83.

14. Speech by Richard M. Nixon, August 23, 1972 (quoted from press release).

15. Speech by Russell B. Long, December 14, 1971 (quoted from a Senate Committee on Finance print).

16. Speech by Russell B. Long, March 14, 1972 (quoted from a Senate Committee on Finance print).

17. Quoted in May, *The Wasted Americans*, p. 18.

18. Speech by George Champion, *Vital Speeches*, xxxiv (December 1, 1967), 113.

19. May, *The Wasted Americans*, p. 13.

20. Robert E. Lane, *Political Ideology* (New York: Free Press, 1962), p. 72.

21. May, *The Wasted Americans*, p. 170.

22. Robert Coles, *The Middle Americans* (Boston: Little, Brown and Co., 1971), p. 102.

23. *Ibid.*, p. 138.

24. Quoted in Gilbert Y. Steiner, *The State of Welfare* (Washington, D.C.: The Brookings Institution, 1971), p. 49.

2
The Historical Background

Negative attitudes toward the poor are not new. Indeed, the ideological props for contemporary attitudes date from the Protestant Reformation. Medieval Christianity had a clear place for the poor in its world view, for charity was regarded as a right of the poor and an important Christian duty of the affluent. This charitable impulse could be seen in the routinization of almsgiving at the parish level and in the development of corporate forms of charity under Catholic auspices such as monastic almsgiving, hospitals, and orphanages. These institutional efforts were often not continued or inaugurated by early Protestants, however, for the Protestant concern with the individual Christian and with work as a calling brought about a de-emphasis on institutionalized charity under church auspices. Emergent Protestant thought brought a new burden for Europe's poor, replacing the benevolent paternalism of Catholicism with a variable, but usually harsh, morality of Protestantism. Many Protestant leaders were, at best, suspicious of the poor and were convinced that individual immorality was the key issue in dealing with poverty. Maintaining the work incentive of the poor was a critical concern. Niebuhr underscored this contrast between Catholicism and early Protestantism:

Whatever the weaknesses of institutional charity from the perspective of the total ethical and social problems of society, it is difficult to escape the conclusion that the superiority of Catholicism over Protestantism in this field of religious activity represents a real virtue of Catholicism—its sense of responsibility for the social realities and the high type of ethical insight developed by the monastic movement. Lutheran Protestantism tends to be Quietistic rather than socially active and the superior social activity of the churches of Calvinism stops short of deep concern for the most needy. Calvinism has never been able to overcome the temptation to regard poverty as a consequence of laziness and vice, and therefore to leave the poor and the needy to the punishment which a righteous God has inflicted upon them.[1]

Under Protestantism the ideology of individualism, sometimes labeled the "work ethic" or the "Protestant ethic," developed as a major Western belief system.

A few important Protestant leaders, particularly Martin Luther and Ulrich Zwingli, did play a role in the development of strict relief arrangements in a number of European municipalities, but these programs were usually small-scale, under civil jurisdiction, and in line with the Protestant ethic. Moreover, the motivation often seems to have been political rather than religious; some sixteenth-century European leaders, religious and secular, had become concerned with the growing class of mobile laborers created by economic shifts and agricultural changes and viewed poor relief as immunization against political unrest.[2] This political concern can be seen in the development of relief laws and programs in England, the shape of which also clearly reflects the impact of Protestant, particularly Calvinist, views of the poor.

IDEOLOGY AND POOR RELIEF
IN ENGLAND

Before the sixteenth century many citizens of England were poor by any definition, so the focus of public assistance programs was on the destitute poor, those in extreme need. English communities relied heavily on private aid, particularly the charity of Catholic parishes and charitable organizations, for support of the destitute. In the late Middle Ages the government's concern with poverty was limited to people vaguely defined as "vagrants" and with the insubordination and destitution which allegedly accompanied vagrancy. The few secular laws relating to the poor, primarily vagrancy and settlement laws, concentrated on keeping propertyless men and women under the domination of the feudal hierarchy. The poor as a group were not a major concern of government in this period, for it was assumed that the Church would provide whatever help was necessary.[3]

With the sixteenth century came an acceleration of change in English social and economic life. Resurgent population growth was beginning to have an impact. This was a period of "special economic stress, whether we emphasize the agrarian revolution that was dislocating the manorial organization, or the growth of manufactures in the towns, involving the production of an urban proletariat; or the rapid increase of commerce, with its unsettlement of one national industry after another."[4] Agrarian reorganization and manufacturing development, with its cycles of employment, were creating a large class of wandering laborers. The rise of a mobile and increasingly urban proletariat led to far more flux in social organization than most members of the ruling elite and the middle classes could tolerate; there was rapidly growing anxiety about and discussion of the link between migration and social disorganization, disorder, and crime; this concern was replete with stereotyping of the poor, for the ruling-class view had begun to shift.

Religious changes were also occurring in this period. By the middle of the sixteenth century Roman Catholicism was being replaced by the English brand of Protestantism, and the Puritan movement was emerging. The views of leading Protestants reinforced negative ruling-class views of the poor; this influence would become particularly conspicuous in the late sixteenth and early seventeenth centuries. The orientation of the English ruling class toward repression in the face of widespread labor mobility and discontent (including riots among the poor) was supported by the Protestant reaction against medieval conceptions of the poor and the Calvinist persistence in seeing poverty as indicative of personal immorality and lack of effort.

For two centuries prior to the rule of King Henry VIII, English statutes had become ever more severe in the punishment provided for "vagrants," a vague term which included not only beggars and criminals but also landless wanderers without proper credentials. Punishment included whipping, compulsory service, or imprisonment. These laws were extended in the statutes of Henry VIII and his successors, for restrictions on the movement of the growing working class and the activities of those considered vagrants were now seen as absolutely essential to public order. The Vagrancy Act of 1597 systematically enumerated those considered to be vagrants; the list encompassed certain types of wandering laborers seeking higher wages, fortune-tellers, peddlers, actors, and a number of other categories of the poor.[5] If persons in any of a dozen categories were caught begging, or if they were unable to account for themselves properly, or if they lived a deviant type of life, they could be severely punished. This legislation remained in effect until the eighteenth century, and from time to time new groups of deviants were included in the list. Such laws provided a legal mechanism for punishing those considered seriously deviant or politically threatening by the English ruling class. In addition to the restrictive vagrancy laws, settlement laws seriously interfered with the mobility of poor laborers; many poor persons were thus tied to one community. Migration was usually restricted to temporary absences; migrant workers were required to have the proper credentials legitimizing their mobility. Before the sixteenth century these laws were limited to laborers in husbandry and to domestic servants—in the sixteenth century, however, with the development of poor relief systems came local ordinances preventing the destitute from other areas from taking up residence in a given local community. In 1662, Parliament passed the Law of Settlement and Removal, which effectively restricted most working-class families to the parish to which they originally belonged.[6]

It is in this context of increasingly repressive vagrancy and settlement laws intended mainly to prevent civil disorder that sixteenth-century legislation designed in part to relieve the economic burden of poverty emerged. The English Poor Laws did not grow out of the pattern of organized almsgiving that had characterized the Catholic Church in the previous century, but rather "in the framework of the severe and even sanguinary statutes which Parliament delighted to enact against the wandering vagabond, the idle and disorderly person, the begging impostor, the trickster and the cheat." [7] But the concern of the ruling elites was not so much with Christian duty as with maintaining order. Government control of the mobile but able-bodied worker, as well as the criminal, was deemed more important than government relief to the poor, but both were to a substantial degree a manifestation of *social control.* The decline of religious (Catholic) charitable institutions and the spreading awareness that the vagrancy and settlement laws alone were not sufficient to defuse revolt potential led the government to the first relief laws. In 1531 the English Parliament took the first small step in the direction of relief for the destitute; begging was authorized for those licensed by local officials as incapable of self-support. Those not so certified could be whipped in public for begging. In 1536 an act passed under Henry VIII charged officials in local communities with responsibility for their poor through a local method of collection, although local officials were not authorized to use public funds or to set up a compulsory tax system.[8] These early laws did not establish a poor relief *system;* this was to come later.

It was only in the 1560s that relief for the poor was institutionalized in a law making poor-tax payments by community householders *obligatory.*[9] Subsequently, the more comprehensive 1572 to 1576 Poor Laws spelled out local responsibility, required that local public officials act as overseers, and established a local tax ("poor rate") to provide financing for relief.[10] In the late sixteenth century economic depression again increased the number of the starving and the unemployed, and, in turn, the number of revolts. It was against this background of civil unrest that Parliament again convened to further codify and extend the laws relating to the care of the poor. The famous 1597 to 1601 Elizabethan Poor Laws systematized earlier regulations, again assigning administrative responsibility for the poor to local officials, requiring a local poor tax, and recommending work-oriented apprenticeship programs for children and institutions for the care of destitute adults. The persistent image of the lazy poor could be seen. Work programs were suggested for the able-bodied poor; houses of correction for vagrants and those unwilling to work; outdoor relief and poorhouses for those disabled by illness or age. In addition, close relatives were legally required to provide support for the poor, and the children of the destitute could be placed out as apprentices. Of course, these laws were not immediately implemented; it would take several decades for them to be heeded throughout England. It is noteworthy too that Parliament also provided for private charitable trusts in this period, an action which eventually spurred the development of private philanthropy as a complementary means for relieving destitution.[11]

During the next century the English Poor Laws became the basis for an administrative system that emphasized *local* responsibility and taxation, at first under centralized supervision, but later relatively free from the control of the central government. While poor relief programs tended to change somewhat with variations in the state of the economy, still the plight of poor Englishmen seems to have become worse in the seventeenth century. A "get-tough" policy linked to negative views of the shiftless poor was developing. Vagrancy laws continued to be enforced, and the most restrictive settlement law yet was promulgated in the early 1660s. According to this statute, and for more than a century thereafter, a landless laborer without proper papers could be removed from one area and compelled to return to his or her original area of settlement, no matter what his or her intentions were in moving around. This act further restricted the migration of poor workers seeking better opportunities.[12] It also provided that local officials could remove persons from their communities who might become destitute and thus dependent on the public purse. "The preamble to this act claimed that large numbers of the indigent were moving to those rural localities where relatively more liberal assistance policies obtained."[13] In fact, most were migrating to urban areas with greater economic alternatives. Such a stereotype of the welfare poor was to persist.

Another signal of the harsh view of the poor emerging in the seventeenth century can be seen in the new emphasis on workhouses. In a Protestant country becoming industrialized, the deification of profit-making and hard work led many to advocate forced employment of the unemployed poor. A number of schemes were devised. "Houses of industry," or workhouses, were regarded as one natural solution that might lead to significant savings in poor relief. Few would undertake the stiff regimen in a workhouse willingly; low-wage work outside workhouses would become more acceptable. Although thousands of workhouses were established in the next two centuries and tens of thousands of poor people were incarcerated in them, most were economic failures and within a few decades had become general shelters for all the poor—the disabled as well as the healthy.[14] An even more dramatic demonstration of the new faith in enforced work for the poor can be seen in late seventeenth-century proposals for farming out the poor to private entrepreneurs who were permitted to set up their own workhouses and secure cheap labor; thus for a fixed sum local parishes could be relieved of the institutional burden. Later on, in the eighteenth century, with the acceleration of the Industrial Revolution, parish officials farmed out the poor in new ways. Poor children were apprenticed not only to those looking for cheap domestic servants but also to capitalists in new industries. Poor adults were farmed out to employers in industry and agriculture in return for provision of support. Many parishes "sought to transfer to some employer—if need be, by compulsory allocation—the duty of enforcing labour and discipline on the poor." [15]

Why had the attitude toward the poor and the destitute become ever more harsh and restrictive? Two answers that appear to be complementary have been suggested by analysts of English relief history. On the one hand, there was the continuing fear among the ruling classes of rebellion and revolt. The development of the Poor Laws occurs step by step with development of a sizable class of unattached working men.

In addition, the new emphasis on regimented workhouses and work programs for the poor ("indoor relief"), as well as on residence requirements for relief administered directly to recipients in their homes ("outdoor relief"), can be linked to the growing importance of Puritan thought. The Puritan variant of Calvinism made its weight felt in ruling-class and rank-and-file views. Puritan individualism was compatible with capitalist expansion. Calvinists tended to view poverty as a sin and a crime; it was seen not just as a social condition leading to civil unrest but also as a problem of personal morality. Conjoined with this was a general orientation to work. Influential Calvinist divines emphasized asceticism and hard work in one's chosen calling, rather than the slow accumulation of good works, as the fundamental obligation of the Christian. Industry in commercial and business efforts was given religious sanction. One of the foremost Puritan thinkers was Richard Baxter, who eloquently advocated the doctrines of hard work in a calling and personal abstinence.[16] Hard work was good in itself. Continuous work was seen as a major defense against the sinful temptations of the flesh; the primary objective of work was to glorify God. Idleness was regarded as sin. Those who were unwilling to work industriously showed signs of a "lack of grace."

Not surprisingly, then, the unemployed and the destitute were looked at with increasing disfavor by many Englishmen; even the part-time work of many poor laborers was regarded either as transitional or as problematic. Begging and almsgiving were often vigorously condemned. No wages were too low and no work too menial for a Christian to refuse. The problem of poverty was considered an individual one, both in cause and in cure. This individualistic perspective on the poor and on work permeated the intellectual environment surrounding the workhouse and work relief "reforms" relating to the relief of the poor in the seventeenth century. With the elaboration of this dominant world view also came the idea that societal inequality in wealth was also God-ordained, that the unequal distribution of worldly goods was necessary because of the variation in the virtue and character of men. The structure of the society or societal flaws that led to unemployment were not to be probed. These ideas about poverty and inequality were eventually secularized and became fundamental and enduring components of the individualistic value system.

Although we cannot present a thorough analysis in this brief historical review, it is important to keep in mind that even in this early period there was developing a more radical tradition sympathetic to the problems of the poor and to the eradication of extreme inequality. A few dared to question the extremes of economic inequality and advocated justice to the poor. Quakers, to take an important example, sometimes pressed Parliament for legal reforms to benefit poor beggars and tenants.[17] Quaker tracts advocated relief for the poor. Yet these structure-oriented views were confined to a minority. Indeed, by the time of the American Revolution both

American and British Quakers had by and large come to accept the individualistic ethic, with its heavy accent on thrift and industry. Prominent Quakers even came to equate the destitute poor with the lazy; by 1700 much of the earlier radicalism was gone.

In many ways public actions toward the poor in the eighteenth and nineteenth centuries continued the pattern of the seventeenth century—resulting in an often uncoordinated assortment of repressive and restrictive programs enmeshed in a work ethic rationale. The workhouse movement continued into the 1700s, but as we have noted previously, many workhouses did not make the profit expected and eventually housed all categories of the poor: they were punishment for the lazy, asylums for the deranged, and hospitals for the sick.[18] It was also in this period that farming out the poor by local officials for private support and profit to farmers and capitalist entrepreneurs became more common. In spite of the emphasis on workhouses, small amounts of money were still being granted in most parishes to selected needy residents. The numbers aided were small relative to the need, as was the amount of money doled out. But those receiving outdoor relief came under increasingly intense scrutiny. Attempts were made from time to time by "reformers" to cut down on the number of "undeserving poor" receiving aid. And by the early 1700s several attempts had been made to force persons receiving such relief to wear pauper's badges on their sleeves, a visible symbol of their degraded status. The stigma attached to public relief persisted.

In England the growth of outdoor relief costs had become an increasing source of discontent by the early 1800s. Between 1760 and 1818 the poor tax increased sixfold.[19] The enclosure movement in agriculture, a number of poor harvests, and the periodic unemployment caused by fluctuations in industrialization led to a growing number of needy people and even to rioting by the poor. "The relief system, in short, was expanded in order to absorb and regulate the masses of discontented people uprooted from agriculture but not yet incorporated into industry."[20] A number of rural parishes in England had experimented by the early 1800s with allowance systems directly supplementing the wages of farm laborers in times of economic hardship (the so-called Speenhamland plan) out of poor taxes paid by employers of farm labor, although apparently these wage subsidies were small and were gradually abandoned.[21] By the 1820s and 1830s the growing poor rate had become a matter of national attention, particularly in the growing urban-industrial areas. Parliament appointed a prestigious and subsequently famous Poor Law Commission which investigated the situation and concluded that the existing system was "a bounty on indolence and vice." [22] Thus the Poor Law reforms in the 1830s attempted to reduce outdoor relief, particularly to the able-bodied unemployed, who—it was argued—should be placed in regimented workhouses. Yet the strict reforms advocated in the 1830s did not take hold in most of England. The nineteenth-century relief system continued arrangements of the eighteenth century; even by the middle of the nineteenth century outdoor relief programs represented a major type of aid to the poor.[23]

THE NORTH AMERICAN COLONIES

To a substantial degree the English system of public aid to the poor was copied in the American colonies. Contrary to some propaganda of the seventeenth and later centuries, there was extensive destitution among the European settlers in the new land. From the beginning, colonial leaders faced the problem of economic distress brought on by such factors as old age, illness, and unemployment. Drawing on the relevant portions of the English laws, they wove a patchwork system of relief to the poor. Colonial laws made local governments responsible for the needs of poor families, permitted local officials to exclude the unworthy poor, and provided for the establishment of residence requirements for relief.[24] From New England to the Southern colonies, restrictive laws were established to regulate poverty and its victims.

The complexity and restrictiveness of the colonial laws and customs relating to the poor can be seen in prevailing practices which have been documented for areas such as New England, New York, and Virginia. In New England the Puritan work ethic received a vigorous articulation both in the writings of prominent leaders and in concrete legislation. Industry and thrift were considered critical and poverty a sign of the lack of both. Cotton

Mather wrote that it was "not lawful for a Christian ordinarily to Live without some *Calling*." Hard work in a well-marked calling would preserve a person from falling "into horrible *Snares*, and infinite *Sins*." [25] Hard work was recommended as the antidote for poverty, and for the related problem of immorality as well. Other Puritan leaders echoed these views.

The New England colonies patterned their relief statutes on the English Poor Laws. Their rather limited public assistance systems emphasized strict controls on vagrancy and unemployment, local responsibility for resident paupers, and local taxation. Moreover, New England officials scrutinized the economic status of strangers; shipmasters were required to post bond to cover the possible dependency of passengers. Poor migrants to an area usually endured a waiting period before they could become official residents.[26] Those strangers who appeared to be potential paupers could be requested to leave ("warned out"), then fined or otherwise punished if they refused. "The interesting old English custom of 'warning out' was widely practiced in New England from 1656 on, often for the purpose of avoiding the responsibility for supporting prospective paupers." [27]

Punishment was also provided for those even considered to be idlers or vagrants, a practice again reflecting the impact of the English laws. In seventeenth-century Massachusetts, Rhode Island, and Connecticut there were laws for the imprisonment or whipping of the able-bodied unemployed.[28] As in England, the distinction between poor but honest laborers forced to wander in search of employment and those unemployed because of personal laziness or crime was not systematically made. The stigma and tribulations of the latter were often visited on the honest poor. Indeed, there was a certain ambivalence toward the poor reflected in New England statutes. At the same time paternalistic concern was expressed for the impotent poor who were established residents, punitive sanctions were meted out to the healthy unemployed and to poor strangers.

Yet this generally negative attitude toward the poor was not just a New England phenomenon. The diversity of Protestant backgrounds in the colonies did not seem to reduce the impact of the individualistic ideology. In New York the English, and the Dutch before them, saw pauperism as a serious problem. Strangers were suspect.[29] In the mid-seventeenth century New York City had a legal code that divided the city into parishes and provided for local overseers of the poor and public collection of poor taxes.[30] Subsequent legislation set up a similar system of local responsibility throughout the New York colony. Residence requirements were established, and the removal of those recent migrants who might become dependent on the public purse was permitted. As in the other colonies, the common form of aid was outdoor relief in the form of money and provisions. Cruel actions were sometimes taken to relieve the parish burden of relief, such as the placing of poor children in other families as apprentices and the "binding out" of the adult poor as indentured servants. An explicit stigma was often attached to the acceptance of relief: "Local officials required paupers to wear badges of blue or red cloth with the large letters 'N:Y' sewn on their clothing, without which no assistance would be granted." [31] In Pennsylvania the destitute poor had to wear the letter "P" on one sleeve of their garments.[32] Stigmatizing the destitute in one form or another was characteristic of the actions of officials in many of the colonies, as it would be of relief officials in subsequent centuries.

Similarly, in Virginia parish welfare organization had developed by the late seventeenth century, and initially certain church officials were responsible for collecting taxes and administering the civil poor laws. If children could not be supported by their unemployed parents, they could be "bound out" to other homes, according to a 1645 law.[33] Vagrancy legislation was also implemented.[34] As in the other colonies, there was some provision for the private care of the poor; aid could be paid out by the vestrymen for those poor afflicted with injury, illness, or old age.

By the seventeenth century most of the colonies from New England to the South had civil laws relating to the regulation of relief of the poor. A number of general points about these laws should be noted. The basic system of relief was assumed to be the network of friends and kin of the poor; relatives were expected, if not required, to care for the destitute. In the first century of settlement most public aid was seen as supplementary and took the form of outdoor relief, of direct aid in one's own home or in the homes of friends or relatives. Separate public institutions for the poor, such as almshouses and workhouses, would not be erected, except in a few of the larger towns, until later.

It is also important to note that the American colonists did not reenact all the provisions of the English Poor Laws. In the first century of colonial development such provisions as those for charitable trusts were ignored. Essentially, the colonists borrowed two major sets of English Poor Law provisions—those requiring local governments to assume responsibility for established residents and those providing for the strict exclusion or regulation of those likely to become paupers. "Towns everywhere used their legal prerogatives to exclude the harmless poor, who might someday need support, and suspicious characters, who could disturb their safety and security." [35] The most severe punishment was reserved for dependent strangers, and established residents were often, but not always, treated in a more paternalistic and benevolent fashion. Linked to this variation in aid and punishment was a perspective which vacillated between generosity and cruelty. Perspectives on the poor and on public aid for the poor in this period do not seem as well-formed or as consistently spelled out as they would be later.

In this period attitudes toward the poor were to a substantial degree related to the Protestant religion of many colonists. Religion was an important part of the colonist's life, and the clergy of the period played a critical role in reinforcing prevailing patterns of thought and behavior, as well as in shaping public and private actions taken to relieve or to punish the poor. Protestant leadership sharpened the distinction between the "deserving" and the "undeserving" poor and supported punishment for the latter. Poverty was considered a natural part of the social order, as was wealth, and extreme inequality did not indicate defects in the social system. Adopting earlier ideas, many even saw poverty as a "God-given opportunity for men to do good." [36] Thus the religious view of social order justified secular arrangements—the hierarchy of social ranks and the unequal economic rewards.[37] It also appears that the non-Protestant (e.g., Catholic) leadership of the colonies soon came to espouse essentially the same views, although we have been able to find little available evidence on this issue.

RELIEF IN THE EIGHTEENTH CENTURY

The beginning of urban development and slowly increasing immigration—together with epidemics, hard winters, and occasional depressions—characterized the eighteenth century, making the problem of poverty even more serious in terms of absolute numbers. With the growth of towns and cities came pressure for institutionalization of the destitute. By the mid-eighteenth century some of the larger towns and cities had an all-purpose institution that operated as a combination almshouse, workhouse, and jail. For example, in New York City an institution was established in 1736 with the title "Poor House, Work House, and House of Correction" and a rigorous set of rules worthy of a maximum security prison.[38] As in England, colonial thinking about work-oriented institutions indicated the punitive attitudes that had developed toward the destitute and deviant poor. The workhouse had developed in part to reinforce the migratory and settlement laws, "to discourage the needy stranger from entering the community, and to punish him should he be apprehended."[39] In addition, local residents regarded as criminals, rogues, or idlers were incarcerated in these institutions, the intent being to force the poor to take regular work at prevailing wages, however low they might be. The assumption, again, was that the poor were not work-oriented. Where almshouses and workhouses were differentiated, as in Philadelphia, the workhouse was publicly justified in terms of the danger to public order posed by migrants, while the almshouse was defended as a way of cutting down on public expenditure for the poor.[40]

Yet by the end of the colonial period outdoor relief was still a major type of public aid, because many towns and cities had not actually erected the heralded almshouse or workhouse. Relief was now largely in the hands of civil authorities. The general approach to the poor still "emphasized removal of nonresidents, work and humiliation as a deterrent for idlers and vagabonds, and a politically inspired attention to the lowest poor taxes consistent with local needs."[41] And the aid granted was such as to guarantee severe economic deprivation. Neither the rise of American philanthropy in this period—which resulted in the establishment of some private charitable organizations, hospitals, and immigrant associations—nor the official recognition of the need for reform of public relief could change this basic image. From the colonial period to the present this country has indeed been a reluctant welfare state.

THE NINETEENTH CENTURY

The first few decades of this new nation's history saw a continuation of economic and social change. Depressions and economic instability punctuated a period of slowly increasing urbanization and industrialization. Coupled with a growing migration stream, these changes dramatized the seriousness of poverty in the United States. As in England, the 1820s and 1830s saw public assistance programs in many local areas, particularly cities, on the brink of collapsing under a rising caseload. In the larger towns and cities the size of the multipurpose poorhouses had grown, with a number eventually housing thousands. Outdoor relief remained a primary aid program for most local governments and accounted for a major share of rising relief budgets.[42]

The growing number of poor immigrants, the periodic food riots, the crime obvious in some poor areas, and the strain on public assistance programs—all these factors combined to provide the social crucible within which attitudes toward the poor would become even more negative and inflexible. The prevailing view was still harsh and moralistic and located the major responsibility for poverty in the character of the poor themselves. Although a number of historians have contrasted the nineteenth-century perspective with the benevolence and generosity of the colonial period,[43] a review of the first two centuries of colonial development suggests that the harsh moralism of the nineteenth century might better be seen simply as a logical extension and amplification of earlier views. Perspectives in the seventeenth and eighteenth centuries seem to have been more inconsistent, however, since harsh moralism alternated with a more benevolent attitude. The colonists were on the whole less obsessed—at least in public discussions—with the problem of poverty and had not formulated as systematic an ideology as had developed by the middle of the nineteenth century. By the 1830s many leaders and middle-class citizens had defined urban poverty as a serious social problem demanding a remedy. Many advocates of relief and work programs appeared to see eradication of poverty as a matter of urgent individual responsibility—the poor themselves were blamed for their state. Perhaps most important, public responsibility for relief and assistance was increasingly questioned. Rising taxes for assistance to the poor and the growing influence of the popularized doctrines of such European laissez-faire political economists as Adam Smith reinforced the taxpayer's growing discontent. Industrialization, population growth, depressions, immigration, and even a number of food riots so dramatized the problem that a "hard line" was accentuated in revised public and private programs designed to deal with poverty. The consistency of this view of the poor and its relevance to new programs soon became clear; it was felt that

if the poor had pauperized themselves through drunkenness, impiety, idleness, extravagance, and immorality, public relief would only reinforce such habits; moral reform for the "vicious" poor and work for the idle would cure dependency more quickly than a secure place in the almshouse or a little temporary relief from the overseers.[44]

This thinking manifested itself in a number of concrete ways: in the operation of schools, religious groups, temperance organizations, and in work relief programs. Mohl has carefully described these developments in the state of New York.[45] Schools became particularly important in control and correction; moral training was the basic goal of poorhouse schools and of Sunday schools. The imperatives of the work ethic, coupled with other prevailing middle-class norms, became a standard in the classroom. Supplementing the schools in the strategy for control of the poor were the newly developed missionary and revival efforts. Because many reformers saw the causes of poverty in un-Christian character flaws such as immorality and slothfulness, the solutions were thought to lie in conversion of the poor to the Christian way of hard work and sober living. Temperance reformers also worked diligently to rid the poor of their addiction to alcohol; for them, abstinence was a major solution for the problem of poverty. Yet these activities were not limited to the state of New York; the inclination to provide moral and exhortatory remedies for poverty was characteristic of educational and reform efforts in many other states as well.

The growing emphasis on moral reformation was also reflected in commission deliberations. A number of commissions investigating poverty in this period were critical of existing programs of poor relief, beginning with a Massachusetts legislative committee investigation in 1821.[46] One recurring theme in the analyses of these commissions was that entrenched poverty should not exist in the United States, given what they viewed rather optimistically as a shortage of labor and excellent wages. They were particularly critical of outdoor relief, which was often seen as an open invitation for the "lazy poor" to become permanently dependent on the public dole. Here was the suggestion that public assistance was creating its own problem, a point of view that has remained popular among public officials. This was also the period when the persisting American doctrine that few would prefer work to benevolent public welfare received great attention; so relief had to be made less appealing ("less eligible" in the jargon) than the condition of the lowliest laborer.[47] Such analyses led to repeated calls for cutbacks in outdoor relief. Some even suggested *abolition* of aid to the poor.

Yet the abolition view did not prevail in the nineteenth century. When public action was taken it usually consisted of reductions in outdoor relief or in the provision of work-oriented institutional facilities. Welfare rolls were periodically purged of the "undeserving" poor. Those who were not taken from the rolls, including the disabled and children as well as the able-bodied unemployed, were often compelled to participate in work programs in institutional settings. A trend toward increased use of institutional facilities paralleled the practice in England. Although public institutions did not account for all aid to the poor, incarceration became central to the search for a solution to poverty.[48] Only a few almshouses had existed in the eighteenth century; but it was not until the mid-nineteenth century that their number increased dramatically. Workhouses were usually part of, or closely related to, public almshouses. In many institutions a strict regimen and firm discipline were supplied to mold the character of the indigent. Yet many of these institutions were not efficiently run, in part because of lack of professional training and experience among managers.

Public support for institutionalization was generated, as we have seen, by a desire to economize on poor relief and by the view that the poor would work only if they came to regard relief as punishment.[49] "The influential Quincy report was filled with unqualified testimony on the power of the institution to terrorize the poor and thereby keep them off the relief rolls." [50] The primary threat was hard labor and oppressive living conditions. As a result, many almshouses and workhouses were institutions with little humanitarian provision for the poor. Probably the majority of the poor in institutions could not be regarded as capable of performing profitable work. The obsession with the undeserving poor and with work relief resulted in a serious neglect of numerous categories of the poor, particularly young children, the mentally ill, the disabled, and the aged. The indifference to their suffering can be seen in the appalling conditions in such public facilities. One New York report (on facilities outside New York City) from the 1850s noted that

it is much to be regretted that our citizens manifest so little interest in the condition even of those in their immediate neighborhood. Individuals who take great interest in human suffering whenever it is brought to their notice, never visit them, and are entirely uninformed; that in a county house almost at their own doors, may be found the lunatic suffering for years in a dark and suffocating cell, in summer, and almost freezing in the winter—where a score of children are poorly fed, poorly clothed, and quite untaught—where the poor idiot is half starved and beaten with rods because he is too dull to do his master's bidding—where the aged mother is lying in perhaps her last sickness, unattended by a physician, and with no one to minister to her wants—where the lunatic, and that lunatic, too, a *woman* is made to feel the lash in the hands of a brutal underkeeper—yet these are all to be found—*they all exist in our State.*[51]

Still, few politically influential Americans, by the middle of the nineteenth century, had paid attention to the pleas of the occasional investigation of these matters.

This negative attitude characterized dominant sentiment for the rest of the nineteenth century. Although the Civil War necessarily accelerated public and private relief programs and decreased moralizing in efforts to aid the poor, this interlude was soon forgotten in the rapid industrialization of the next few decades. Immigration, urbanization, and serious depressions were now joined by war dislocation and disability as factors increasing the number of the destitute. Yet it seemed that the more conspicuous these structural conditions came to be in the etiology of poverty in the United States, the more "the American gospel of individualism continued to foster the belief that any hardworking, moral man could support his family in independence and dignity." [52] This positive side of the work ethic continued to be linked to a negative view of the poor. With this attitude and the rising cost of relief, it is not surprising that outdoor relief again came under fire. In the 1870s and 1880s numerous urban governments eliminated it or reduced its availability and came to rely even more than before on public almshouses and private charitable organizations.

Neither the few critics of almshouses nor reports of the deplorable conditions there could divert this reliance on institutionalization. In the last decades of the nineteenth century many of the almshouses were filled with recent immigrants, often from populations considered racially inferior by earlier immigrant groups. This further increased the social distance between the poor and their affluent surroundings. Custodial care remained a major type of care for the poor until well into the twentieth century, although public outdoor relief continued to play a minor role. Beneficial changes in poverty actions seldom occurred. In some northeastern states such as Massachusetts, one important reform development did bring some improvement to the lives of some of the poor. Separate, professionally staffed institutions developed for various specialized categories of the poor, such as the blind and the mentally ill, but such differentiation took place slowly. Even in progressive categorical institutions, however, the "deserving" poor had to submit to a demeaning institutional regimen and conform to strict regulations. Increasingly, too, state boards of charities took control of institutions formerly in the hands of local government; these state boards were the predecessors of later state welfare agencies.

The late nineteenth century also saw an increased reliance on private charitable organizations to aid the poor that was related to the move away from public outdoor relief. Particularly important was the Charity Organization Society (COS) movement, which spread to many cities in the 1870s and 1880s. This COS movement, influenced by the social Darwinism of the time, advocated "scientific charity" and an investigative and counseling approach to the poor emphasizing secular rather than religious reform and anticipating twentieth-century social work practices. By such "personal service" and social counseling the COS advocates felt that the poor could be pressured to help themselves. Not surprisingly, then, by the early 1900s only a modest proportion of local expenditures for the poor in numerous areas went for outdoor relief.[53]

THE GOSPEL OF INDIVIDUALISM

A major reason for the slow progress in humanitarian reform of aid to the poor in the last half of the nineteenth century was, as we have seen, the further elaboration and broad dissemination of the ideology of individualism. After the Civil War this was further buttressed by the doctrines of social Darwinism. The last half of the nineteenth century was a major era of rapid capitalistic expansion in the United States, with an unprecedented exploitation of natural and human resources and the development of new industries. The evolutionary perspective of Charles Darwin, as applied to human society by the social Darwinists, was compatible with this aggressive expansion in its two main themes: the "struggle for survival" and the "survival of the fittest." Social and economic life was considered to be by nature a life-and-death struggle in which the best individual competitors both should and would win out over others. Moreover, the hierarchical structure of society and its socioeconomic or class divisions, including distinctions between the rich and the poor, were also thought to be the result of the operation of basic laws of nature. Closely linked to these beliefs was the further idea that the competitive struggle should not be tampered with by government, lest all manner of social and economic ills result.

Darwin himself had suggested the policy implications of the Darwinist perspective for the disabled and the poor:

We civilized men, on the other hand, do our utmost to check the process of elimination; we build asylums for the imbecile, the maimed, and the sick;

we institute poor-laws; and our medical men exert their utmost skill to save the life of everyone to the last moment. There is reason to believe that vaccination has preserved thousands, who from a weak constitution would formerly have succumbed to small-pox. Thus the weak members of civilized societies propagate their kind. No one who has attended to the breeding of domestic animals will doubt that this must be highly injurious to the race of man. It is surprising how soon a want of care, or care wrongly directed, leads to the degeneration of a domestic race; but excepting in the case of man himself, hardly any one is so ignorant as to allow his worst animals to breed.[54]

The implication of this passage seems clear: it might be better for the human race if the poor, the sick, and the disabled were not aided by private or public means, but allowed to die off.

Social Darwinist thinking about the natural character of ruthless social and economic competition, about the inevitability of poverty, and about the perils of government reform was developed by English thinkers such as Herbert Spencer and soon spread to the United States, where it significantly influenced businessmen, clergymen, and intellectual leaders. "In the late nineteenth century, Conservative Darwinism was standard doctrine in thousands of American pulpits, universities and newspaper offices."[55] Both science and religion now gave legitimacy to an increasingly rigorous ideal of individualism, and numerous prominent leaders utilized the language of social Darwinism in developing their views of the economic scene. James J. Hill, a railroad entrepreneur, argued that "the fortunes of railroad companies are determined by the law of the survival of the fittest and thereby justified railroad monopolies."[56] John D. Rockefeller, one of the wealthiest Americans of his day, took no less an occasion than a Sunday school address to identify aggressive capitalistic competition—an example of which was the Standard Oil Trust—with the laws of nature and of God:

The growth of a large business is merely a survival of the fittest. . . . The American Beauty rose can be produced in the splendor and fragrance which bring cheer to its beholder only by sacrificing the early buds which grow up around it. This is not an evil tendency in business. It is merely the working-out of a law of nature and a law of God.[57]

Andrew Carnegie reported that reading social Darwinist theories had contributed to his peace of mind. From his vantage point the existence of poverty in societies was healthy, because the greatest men of the human race had been molded in the "school of poverty." Those who did not learn this lesson of genius from the "school of poverty" were morally inferior. For Carnegie, as for the other capitalists of this period, the existence of both wealth and poverty was grounded in the natural order of things.[58]

William Graham Sumner, one of the most famous intellectuals and business advocates of his day, was also articulate and influential in his speeches and writings. He argued vigorously that wealthy industrialists and financiers were the true creators not only of wealth in this society but also of human virtue.[59] The wealthy were products of natural selection and essential to the advance of civilization. The poor and the destitute, however, were a drag on evolutionary development. In line with Darwin's view of society, Sumner scoffed at sentimentalists who

seem to be terrified that distress and misery still remain on earth and promise to remain as long as the vices of human nature remain. Many of them are frightened at liberty, especially under the form of competition, which they elevate into a bugbear. They think it bears harshly on the weak. They do not perceive that here "the strong" and "the weak" are terms which admit of no definition unless they are made equivalent to the industrious and the idle, the frugal and the extravagant. They do not perceive, furthermore, that if we do not like the survival of the fittest, we have only one possible alternative, and that is the survival of the unfittest. The former is the law of civilization; the latter is the law of anti-civilization.[60]

Not surprisingly, he was generally opposed to governmental interference in this natural social and economic process. Adamantly opposed to poor relief, which in his view enabled the weak to survive and consume resources needed elsewhere, he amplified the exhortatory moralism characteristic of earlier centuries in his solution for poverty: "Let every man be sober, industrious, prudent, and wise, and bring up his children to be so likewise, and poverty will be abolished in a few generations." [61]

Thus social Darwinism, with its scientific aura, further sanctified the work ethic that had been nurtured in the Reformation and further nourished in the ascetic Protestantism of the seventeenth and eighteenth centuries. The shift in emphasis from the laws of God to the laws of nature could be seen in much discussion of the day. But the hero was still the competitive individualist who lived an industrious and temperate life. Magazine articles, newspaper stories, sermons, the lectures of educators, the speeches of businessmen, and the "rags-to-riches" books of writers such as Horatio Alger—all these combined to circulate the ideas of the triumph of individual effort, the victory of work over circumstance, and the ignominy of poverty. Sumner and his fellow social Darwinists thus helped to bridge the historical period between the work ethic of the Protestant reformers and the ideologies of the twentieth century.[62]

In addition to social Darwinism, other factors should be noted as contributing to the development of the ideology of individualism in the late nineteenth century. The impact of European economists has already been noted. Of particular importance were the frontier conditions, which fostered a "rugged individualism," a dependence on individual effort, and self-reliance.[63]

The late nineteenth century was a period of individualism run rampant. The consequences of a work-oriented ideology of individualism reinforced by the rigorous philosophical rationale of social Darwinism were quite serious for the poor—as a result, they were attacked vigorously from all corners of the society. Religious and moral justifications for inequality and misery had been basic to American thought for some time, but now with "scientific" sanction they became even more resistant to change. The likelihood of major governmental programs to aid the poor became increasingly remote, for efforts such as progressive reform were seen as efforts to destroy the very progress of Western civilization.

THE TWENTIETH CENTURY

The nineteenth-century reluctance to engage in significant welfare reform other than that aimed at saving taxpayer dollars persisted into the twentieth century. Few leaders in the new industrial economy seemed willing to make major concessions in the direction of expanded public assistance for the poor. Many Americans had been persuaded to agree with this reluctance. Although the period between 1900 and 1920 brought new pressure for reform from muckraking journalists, crusading social workers, and other activists, the concrete reforms that ultimately resulted— workmen's compensation laws, laws regulating the working conditions of women and children, tenement house regulations—were limited and often rather weak in that they left many in the working classes uncovered and did not deal with the basic problems of underemployment or unemployment.[64] In addition, middle-class reformers of the period were concerned with the plight of small entrepreneurs and put a lot of effort into reforms dealing with the ever-expanding business monopolies and government corruption; these efforts did lead to some modest corporate reform, but the poor profited only a little, because most benefits went to classes above the level of the very poor.

Beyond this limited protective legislation, some of which was actually rescinded in the 1920s, relatively little was done in the first two decades to change the basic shape of the restrictive system of aid to the poor. In most areas state and locally administered public institutions for categories of the destitute continued to be a key part of the assistance system, supplemented by private charity and periodic tinkering with outdoor relief. Of course, this was a period of increased interest in studying poverty with applied social science methods, a development generated by the "scientific charity" orientation of COS and other private charity movements.

Public outdoor relief increasingly became more important in the decade or so prior to the Great Depression, but the restrictive orientation toward the poor persisted. Categorical distinctions were a main feature of the modest new programs. Under pressure from some reformers and influential settlement house workers, a handful of states made an attempt to foster, but not require, local old-age assistance programs; most of these were optional and financed solely out of local funds; consequently, only 1,000 elderly persons were receiving assistance by 1929.[65] So the almshouse continued to be the last resort for the aged poor. By 1930 some states had also provided similar legislation for the blind. In addition, by that time a majority of states had made some legislative provision for "pension" programs for needy mothers with children. The earliest laws governing such programs were restrictive. Some permitted juvenile courts the option of ordering local governments to support needy young children in homes. Of course, instead of providing home aid, the courts could still place a needy child in an institution. And some programs limited such aid to widows. Moreover, mother's aid programs were often explicitly discussed in social control terms, with an emphasis on issues such as the prevention of immorality. Even these assistance programs were generally not mandatory and generally provided *no* state or federal government aid; as a result they were implemented in relatively few counties and cities—where they were, assistance payments were quite low. The mothers who qualified were often expected to submit to a humiliating investigation and subsequently to social casework, a diagnostic and counseling operation which by the late 1920s was growing in importance and in extent of controversy in the social work profession.[66] Nevertheless, these limited local categorical programs were very important precedents for the federally supported public assistance system which developed and spread to most states in the 1930s and 1940s.

In general, the decade of the 1920s was a reactionary period in which the expansion of relief to the poor was a low priority at all levels of government. Progressive achievements for the average worker were constantly in danger of being rolled back. Corporate influence increased, and the various regulatory agencies established under the auspices of the earlier reformers often fell into the hands of business interests. The relatively restricted old-age, blind, and mother's pension programs limped along, constantly under threat of judicial revocation.

The suggestion of some Progressives that a structural perspective on the poor might be more adequate than the traditional individualistic perspective was largely forgotten. The view that social and economic conditions were more important than individual morality in explaining poverty, what Bremner has termed a "new view" of poverty,[67] was limited to a few lonely academic and social work advocates crying in an individualistic wilderness. For most American leaders and middle-income Americans poverty was not a critical public issue. Indeed, some believed that the reforms of the first two decades had essentially abolished it. Many believed with the Republican presidents and leaders of the 1920s that rugged individualism and voluntary charity at the local level could carry Americans through economic troubles, whether they were personal or societal. There was thought to be no need for additional *federal* government involvement, for joint action by voluntary charity and local relief agencies should be sufficient for community problems of poverty. Indeed, even the first years of the Great Depression did not shake the faith of most in the ruling elites that federal governmental interference was unnecessary to meet the needs of the growing number of citizens thrown into a state of destitution by a seriously malfunctioning economy.

THE GREAT DEPRESSION

As the Depression became more serious and the country moved into the 1930s, more and more leaders came to see that this radically new type of economic crisis required some type of increased government action. At first, emphasis was placed on the state and local levels. Slowly, however, business, government, and academic leaders alike called for federal involvement, if only to protect the interests of the ruling class. The inability of local relief agencies, both private charity organizations and new public agencies, to cope with accelerating unemployment and poverty by themselves—and the eventual bankruptcy of many such agencies—made federal intervention inevitable. The idea, moreover, that private charitable organizations could be the primary backstop for local public relief in times of crisis became, for the time being at least, increasingly suspect.

Demands from those hit hardest by unemployment and declining farm incomes for economic intervention by the national government and for an expansion of direct monetary assistance for the needy became ever more strident. There was a growing threat to public order: "Groups of men out of work congregated at local relief agencies, cornered and harassed administrators, and took over offices until their demands were met—which usually meant that money or goods were distributed to them." [68] Protest organizations, rent strikes, and large demonstrations had an impact on business and government leaders. Demands from local and state agencies for federal money to meet their ever growing public assistance costs also escalated.

Relief for the needy and the unemployed was soon forthcoming, clearly a response to intensified grass-roots pressure. One of the first federal programs to reach large numbers of the jobless was that administered by the Federal Emergency Relief Administration (FERA). By the end of 1934 direct unemployment relief, administered through state and local agencies, had reached one-sixth of the population, although the average monthly payments were small. FERA provided cash support for state and local programs. A surplus commodities program was also established at this time under FERA auspices. However, as the panic and unrest decreased somewhat, so did the federal government's emphasis on direct relief.[69] Increasingly, New Deal programs emphasized work relief programs, some of which had originated under FERA auspices. During the middle years of the 1930s a large number of work-oriented programs were gradually implemented (some had been inaugurated earlier) to meet the needs of the army of the able-bodied unemployed. The New Deal developed such government-subsidized programs as the Civilian Conservation Corps, the Public Works Administration, the National Youth Administration, and the Works Progress Administration—all of which helped to provide billions of dollars in job aid for millions of jobless workers.

Yet support for large-scale federal intervention in the economy of this type proved to be temporary and limited. In spite of the need demonstrated by unprecedented economic dislocation, opposition to federal aid was always extensive in the 1930s. In particular, direct monetary relief continued to be suspect for many; prominent taxpayers and newspapers continued to espouse the traditional suspicion of the poor, the rigid moralism that had characterized dominant views for several centuries:

Indeed, taxpayers often expressed the view that those on direct relief were getting nothing less than a soul-destroying handout, and for the duration of the depression Americans vastly preferred work relief to cash relief. In city after city, investigations were staged to weed out welfare "chiselers" and newspapers railed against "boondogglers" and "shirkers." [70]

Even President Franklin Roosevelt, from time to time, felt compelled to criticize direct monetary relief as compared to work relief. As the years passed, many Americans even came to question the work-oriented relief programs. National opinion polls showed that resistance to governmental interference in economic matters remained extensive even in hard times. By the late 1930s public opinion polls revealed that a majority felt that communities should *reduce* relief spending. In another important opinion poll, negative evaluations of relief programs such as the Works Progress Administration (WPA) now exceeded positive evaluations.[71] By the late 1930s newspapers had accelerated their attack on welfare problems and graft, while middle-income homeowners had begun a taxpayers' revolt against rising property taxes and relief expenditures.

In addition to negative expressions of taxpayer opinion about various New Deal relief programs, there was also constant political attack from Republicans and other conservatives, including those in administrative positions at local and state government levels. Numerous problems of implementation and local resistance developed, sometimes reflecting jurisdictional squabbles between levels of government, sometimes involving fundamental ideological disagreement. Implementation difficulties were exacerbated by the position of the opposition party. The Republican party persistently attacked direct federal relief programs and called for return of the "relief business" solely to the control of local authorities. Influenced by conservative and business interests, Congress cut back New Deal cash relief and employment assistance programs well before the economy had the ability to provide jobs for most of the unemployed.

Perhaps the most important effect of the persisting ideology of individualism and of opposition to expansion of the public assistance system could be seen in the day-to-day operation of Depression relief programs. From the beginning, cash relief payments were quite low. Local city programs were often victimized by stingy state legislatures, work relief never came close to meeting the unemployment need, and local assistance agencies were chronically understaffed. In addition, many public social workers harbored individualistic, and even punitive, attitudes. Because of governmental reluctance, most needing relief had been denied aid; indeed, it has been estimated in regard to public works programs that "for every person on the federal payroll, at least four had been denied relief." [72] Although it was clear that a complex bureaucratic structure at several levels of government had developed in the 1930s to deal with welfare needs and the poor, it also seems evident that the changes were modest in comparison to the need. Nor did some programs last long. Direct relief under FERA was soon cut back, and work relief barely survived until 1941. Once the pressure was off, Congress returned to a position more in line with the traditional ideology of individualism.

THE SOCIAL SECURITY ACT

With the demise of direct relief and work relief programs, the relief revolution of the 1930s came to an end. Only one major piece of New Deal relief legislation, the 1935 Social Security Act, survived. Although most of the New Deal's relief agencies were gone by World War II, the programs that grew out of the major provisions of the Social Security Act have become the backbone of the contemporary welfare system. As finally passed, the Social Security Act set up a federally financed and administered old-age insurance program; a state-regulated unemployment insurance program financed by payroll taxes; and a federally assisted and state (and locally) administered public assistance program. In the next chapter we will examine the broader context, the purposes, and the structure of public assistance programs in greater detail. The reader should note that, in providing extensive financial aid for these latter programs, the federal government was again acting to bail out hard-pressed state and local government aid programs.

Even this modest step in the direction of aid for working Americans was taken against great opposition. Although the programs of social insurance were supported by leading officials in the Roosevelt Administration and by many working-class Americans, there was extensive opposition to the pending legislation from influential groups. Business and local government officials expressed the fear that such proposals would destroy individual initiative, although some eventually came to see that some action was necessary to shut off protest and forestall radical reform. Once the

Act was finally passed, its difficulties were not over, for the Supreme Court did not validate its constitutionality until 1937. In an historic decision the Supreme Court argued that the "Congress may spend money in and for the general welfare." [73] Moreover, the programs as established also had major weaknesses. The social insurance programs established for aged and unemployed workers were limited in a number of ways. Large categories of workers were not covered. Old-age benefits were not paid until 1942. Unemployment insurance was controlled by the states, so both payments and waiting periods could vary greatly. Both programs had substantial prior work requirements, so chronically unemployed workers in the labor force often could not benefit from these programs.[74]

Was there a "welfare state revolution" revealed in the social insurance and public assistance actions taken during the Depression? Assertions of this type seem to be gross exaggerations of the truth, for the programs did not begin to meet the needs of the millions of poor persons. Indeed, the weaknesses of the Social Security Act prompted one prominent social worker to evaluate it as a law designed "to furnish such means of security as provoked no serious opposition." [75] Of course, as we shall see in the next chapter, many leaders viewed the public assistance programs as a *temporary* liability for federal, state, and local governments, expecting this obligation to be replaced eventually by work and family institutions. This legislation did mark a shift in the direction of the acknowledgment of some *federal responsibility* for relief of the poor, and in this sense it might be accurately described as a "significant break with past restrictions and inhibitions." [76] Yet in spite of these significant changes in administrative and funding patterns, the underlying philosophy and rationale of public assistance programs had not changed. An emphasis on individualism and on moral reform of the poor persisted.

1. Reinhold Niebuhr, *The Contribution of Religion to Social Work* (New York: Columbia University Press, 1932), pp. 15–16.

2. Sidney Webb and Beatrice Webb, *English Poor Law History*, Part 1: *The Old Poor Law* (London: Frank Cass and Co., Ltd., 1963), pp. 31–33.

3. *Ibid.*, p. 396.

4. *Ibid.*, p. 43.

5. *Ibid.*, pp. 351–52.

6. *Ibid.*, pp. 314–16.

7. *Ibid.*, p. 350.

8. Frances Fox Piven and Richard A. Cloward, *Regulating the Poor* (New York: Pantheon Books, 1971), p. 15.

9. Webb and Webb, *English Poor Law History*, p. 51.

10. Piven and Cloward, *Regulating the Poor*, pp. 15–16.

11. Raymond A. Mohl, "Three Centuries of American Public Welfare: 1600–1932," *Current History*, 65 (July 1973), 6; Blanche D. Coll, *Perspectives in Public Welfare* (Washington, D.C.: U.S. Government Printing Office, 1969), pp. 4–7.

12. Webb and Webb, *English Poor Law History*, pp. 315–30.

13. Coll, *Perspectives in Public Welfare*, pp. 7–8.

14. *Ibid.*, p. 8.

15. Webb and Webb, *English Poor Law History*, p. 400.

16. Max Weber, *The Protestant Ethic and the Spirit of Capitalism*, transl. Talcott Parsons (New York: Scribner's, 1958), pp. 155–61, 177–78, and notes on pp. 263–68. On Puritan individualism and capitalist expansion, see R. H. Tawney, *Religion and the Rise of Capitalism* (New York: Mentor Books, 1954), pp. 98–106.

17. Hugh Barbour, *The Quakers in Puritan England* (New Haven: Yale University Press, 1964), pp. 171–250.

18. This paragraph draws heavily on Webb and Webb, *English Poor Law History*, pp. 161, 218–20.

19. Piven and Cloward, *Regulating the Poor*, pp. 19–21.

20. *Ibid.*, p. 21.

21. Coll, *Perspectives in Public Welfare*, pp. 10–11; Webb and Webb, *English Poor Law History*, pp. 177–80; Piven and Cloward, *Regulating the Poor*, pp. 29–30. We do not discuss the Speenhamland plan further because currently not enough is known about its extent.

22. Cited in Coll, *Perspectives in Public Welfare*, p. 11.

23. *Ibid.*, pp. 11–12.

24. David J. Rothman, *The Discovery of the Asylum* (Boston: Little, Brown and Company, 1971), pp. 20–21.

25. Cotton Mather, "A Christian at His Calling," in *The American Gospel of Success*, ed. Moses Rischin (Chicago: Quadrangle Books, 1965), p. 24.

26. Neil Betten, "American Attitudes toward the Poor: A Historical Overview," *Current History*, 65 (July 1973), p. 2.

27. Marcus W. Jernegan, *Laboring and Dependent Classes in Colonial America, 1607–1783* (Chicago: University of Chicago Press, 1931), p. 193.

28. *Ibid.*, p. 200; also Betten, "American Attitudes toward the Poor," p. 2.

29. Betten, "American Attitudes toward the Poor," p. 2.

30. Raymond A. Mohl, *Poverty in New York, 1783–1825* (New York: Oxford University Press, 1971), pp. 41–42.

31. *Ibid.*, p. 42.

32. Edgar May, *The Wasted Americans* (New York: Signet Books, 1964), p. 16.

33. Betten, "American Attitudes toward the Poor," p. 2.

34. Jernegan, *Laboring and Dependent Classes in Colonial America, 1607–1783*, pp. 175–88.

35. Rothman, *The Discovery of the Asylum*, p. 46.

36. *Ibid.*, p. 7.

37. *Ibid.*, p. 10.

38. Mohl, *Poverty in New York, 1783–1825*, p. 45.

39. Rothman, *The Discovery of the Asylum*, p. 25.

40. *Ibid.*, pp. 26–28.

41. Mohl, *Poverty in New York, 1783–1825*, p. 51.

42. Mohl, "Three Centuries of American Public Welfare: 1600–1932," p. 7.

43. See Walter I. Trattner, "Private Charity in America: 1700–1900," *Current History*, 65 (July 1973), 25–28.

44. Mohl, "Three Centuries of American Public Welfare: 1600–1932," p. 9.

45. Mohl, *Poverty in New York, 1783–1825*, pp. 173–201.

46. Rothman, *The Discovery of the Asylum*, pp. 157–65.

47. Mohl, "Three Centuries of American Public Welfare: 1600–1932," p. 8.

48. *Ibid.*, pp. 8–9.

49. Rothman, *The Discovery of the Asylum*, pp. 180–202.

50. *Ibid.*, p. 195.

51. Coll, *Perspectives in Public Welfare*, pp. 26–27.

52. Mohl, "Three Centuries of American Public Welfare: 1600–1932," p. 9.

53. *Ibid.*, pp. 9–10; also Coll, *Perspectives in Public Welfare*, pp. 43–56.

54. Charles Darwin, *The Origin of the Species and the Descent of Man* (New York: Modern Library, 1936), p. 501.

55. Eric F. Goldman, *Rendezvous with Destiny* (New York: Vintage Books, 1956), p. 71.

56. Quoted in Richard Hofstadter, *Social Darwinism in American Thought*, rev. ed. (Boston: Beacon Press, 1955), p. 45.

57. Quoted in *ibid.*, p. 45.

58. *Ibid.*, pp. 45–46.

59. *Ibid.*, pp. 55–66.

60. Quoted in *ibid.*, p. 57.

61. Quoted in *ibid.*, p. 61.

62. *Ibid.*, p. 51.

63. Dorothy B. James, *Poverty, Politics, and Change* (Englewood Cliffs, N.J.: Prentice-Hall, Inc., 1972), p. 28.

64. See "Introduction," in *The Progressive Years*, ed. Otis Pease (New York: George Braziller, 1962), pp. 1–22.

65. Coll, *Perspectives in Public Welfare*, p. 81.

66. *Ibid.*, pp. 76–80; also Joel F. Handler and Ellen J. Hollingsworth, *The "Deserving Poor"* (Chicago: Markham Publishing Co., 1971), pp. 20–24.

67. Robert H. Bremner, *From the Depths* (New York: New York University Press, 1966), pp. 124–26.

68. Piven and Cloward, *Regulating the Poor*, pp. 61–62.
69. *Ibid.*, pp. 72–80.
70. Charles H. Trout, "Welfare in the New Deal Era," *Current History*, 65 (July 1973), 12.
71. *Ibid.*, p. 13.
72. *Ibid.*, p. 39.
73. Charles I. Schottland, *The Social Security Program in the United States* (New York: Appleton-Century-Crofts, 1963), pp. 38–39.
74. Piven and Cloward, *Regulating the Poor*, p. 114.
75. Bremner, *From the Depths*, p. 264.
76. Schottland, *The Social Security Program in the United States*, p. 39.

3

The Welfare System

A recent addition to the vocabularies of analysts of Western societies has been the expression "welfare state," a term usually reserved for describing the growth of government concern for the economic and physical well-being of its citizens. The rise of the welfare state has been analyzed by numerous learned observers. Rostow praises it as a manifestation of society's economic and technical maturity.[1] Myrdal also sees it as good that the countries of the Western world have become democratic welfare states with clear governmental commitment to the "broad goals of economic development, full employment, equality of opportunity for the young, social security, and protected minimum standards as regards not only income, but nutrition, housing, health, and education for people of all regions and social groups." [2]

One accented theme among some of these analysts is the dramatic progress the United States has made since the 1930s in redistributional reform, particularly in social security, social insurance, and related programs for workers and in the establishment of a public assistance floor for the poor. Indeed, the 1930s have been heralded as the beginning of government action which moved the United States significantly in the direction of economic redistribution. One prominent liberal economist, who sees the present welfare state in the United States as a significant break with the past and as a move toward greater economic equality, is of the opinion that this welfare state "will long be with us." [3]

Other analysts, however, express concern over the slow pace of welfare state development. Wilensky and Lebeaux have described the United States as the "most reluctant welfare state" in its expansion of governmental concern.[4] Other observers remain unconvinced that the much-touted welfare state is any more than a meager *substitute* for significant changes in the distribution of major economic benefits.[5] From this viewpoint the rhetoric of redistribution has not been matched by the wealth, resource, or organizational shifts that could lead to a significant decrease in economic inequality. Richard Edwards agrees that the last few decades have seen an increase in welfare and anti-poverty programs, but maintains that "they have had a minuscule impact on the distribution of income in the United States." [6] Even liberals seem more concerned with a minimum subsistence floor for the poor than with redistribution of wealth.

Some analysts convincingly argue that, whatever else it may have accomplished, the United States' version of the welfare state has not significantly affected, in the last three decades, the overall structure of economic inequality. This can be seen in data on the proportion of total before-tax family income going to each fifth of American families:[7]

	1947	1955	1969
Lowest fifth	5%	5%	6%
Second fifth	12	12	12
Third fifth	17	18	18
Fourth fifth	23	24	23
Highest fifth	43	42	41
	100%	101% *	100%

* Due to rounding.

The lowest 20 percent of American families, in terms of income, received only about 5 percent of the *total* family income in 1947, compared to 43 percent for the highest-income fifth. Remarkably, this unequal distribution changed only slightly over the two "welfare state" decades since 1947. This picture of inequality would probably be more dramatic if total wealth, not just current income, were taken into consideration, and this would likely be the case if the economic worth of benefits in kind could be calculated. However, it may well be that although welfare state programs have not significantly redistributed economic benefits, they may have actually retarded a built-in movement in capitalist societies toward even greater inequality; but this is an issue which, apparently, no analyst has probed.

THE CONTEXT OF WELFARE FOR
THE POOR: SUBSIDIES FOR ALL

Few would disagree that over the last few decades the federal government has substantially expanded its intervention in the economic sphere. Although liberals stress the beneficial effect of welfare state activity on economic inequality, this effect may be greatly exaggerated, and thus we must ask what this federal involvement has done. The answer to this important question appears to lie in the vast array of subsidies provided by federal, state, and local governments for income classes above the poverty line. This aid has aptly been termed "welfare for the affluent."

The irony of this type of aid can be seen in one story that appeared in the late 1960s. A news report revealed that James Eastland, a conservative Senator from Mississippi and a critic of welfare, had received more than $150,000 in federal subsidy payments in 1967 for keeping his land idle.[8] In that same year an average Mississippi mother who could not find employment could not receive more than $500 in federally subsidized welfare aid for herself and her family. The senator's need for government relief was seen as legitimate, while the welfare mother's was deemed illegitimate. "Our welfare systems do not distribute benefits on the basis of need. Rather they distribute benefits on the basis of legitimacy."[9] And legitimacy seems to be closely related to the amount of wealth and power a group or class already has at its disposal. Although some examples of large government subsidies to the wealthy have occasionally appeared in the mass media in recent years, little publicity has been given to the fact that *many* businesses and *many* nonpoor Americans receive government "handouts" or subsidies in one form or another. Yet few are aware of the magnitude of these direct and indirect economic benefits. Indeed, these governmental subsidies have been estimated at $60 to 70 billion.[10]

For example, billions in aid go each year to American businessmen and industrialists in the form of agricultural subsidies to farmers; investment tax credits for businesses; large subsidies or loan guarantees to ship builders, aircraft companies, and railroads; indirect subsidies to resource industries (such as substantial tax relief for the oil industry); and substantial tax relief for investors.[11] Much of this aid does not take the form of direct government spending, but rather is made possible by the existence of tax loopholes, resulting in large savings for some and increased taxes for others. One observer has wryly noted that "there are no more persistent and successful applicants for public assistance than the proud giants of the private enterprise system."[12]

Under the beneficent system allowing various subsidies to middle- and upper-income taxpayers, homeowners can deduct mortgage interest charges, donors can deduct gifts, and married couples get special tax advantages. Persons in all income classes benefit from these tax subsidies, but those who are relatively well-off tend to receive the greatest benefits. Then there are programs like Social Security—because it is viewed as social insurance, it is a program with the trappings of legitimacy. In theory, it is a scheme by which workers contribute while working and receive their earned benefits later; but on the average, the benefits are several times what a worker has paid in. In addition, taxes on those currently employed support those who are now retired. Moreover, it has been suggested that even this subsidy program mainly benefits nonpoor Americans.[13] Some redistribution may have taken place within the middle levels of this society, but in the last few decades there has been no major redistribution from the very affluent to the destitute.

The Dual Subsidy System. The United States now has a dual subsidy system. One part of the system, the government aid discussed above, is seldom thought of as a subsidy or welfare program and is seen as legitimate. The other part of the dual system, public assistance, is considered to be a government welfare program and is often viewed as wholly or partially illegitimate. Common terms—"welfare," "relief," the "dole"—point up the stigma of illegitimacy attached to public assistance. The fully legitimate subsidy programs differ from public assistance in providing more liberal benefits, in being covered by a legitimating rhetoric, and in being better concealed from public scrutiny.[14] The quasi-legitimate subsidies, public assistance programs, are usually local or state controlled, provide less in the way of direct and side benefits, and involve more societal intervention into private lives. In addition, the less egalitarian subsidy programs, aid for business and industry and even Social Security, have historically been the most favored; the most truly egalitarian programs, such as public assistance, have historically been starved.

Welfare and Its Goals. Given the traditional stigma attached to welfare in the dual system, a question inevitably arises as to the goals of welfare. What are the traditional aims of public assistance? What have assistance programs accomplished, or at least attempted to accomplish? Our review of the historical background and development of the American welfare system in Chapter 2 pointed up a number of manifest and hidden goals that have characterized poor relief for centuries. Drawing on this material, and on that which follows in this chapter, we would suggest that at least the following major goals or purposes have characterized the American welfare system:

1. To relieve the suffering of the destitute poor (usually at minimum cost);
2. To maintain the existing political and economic order (a) by expanding public relief somewhat in times of protest and (b) by utilizing public assistance to encourage or insure maximum work effort from key groups among the very poor;
3. To reform the work attitudes and morals of the very poor.

More recently, a fourth goal has been given some emphasis, that of rehabilitation. In a sense this purpose is derivative, because the intent behind rehabilitation programs seems to be closely related to the three traditional purposes listed above.

The goals of the welfare system constitute a paradoxical mixture of charitable impulses and concern for the maintenance of social order. Some purposes have been widely discussed, while others have remained relatively hidden. Concern for suffering has been evident. In the 1930s the congressional discussion of public assistance for the aged, the blind, and mothers with dependent children emphasized relief of the suffering of the destitute, although there were also numerous statements reflecting concern with the consequences of programs for the morals of the poor. Subsequently, much discussion of the relief system by welfare administrators and professionals stressed its charitable aspects. Their statements about goals often view the welfare system as protecting the weak, as providing supportive resources for malfunctioning individuals and families, and as enhancing the well-being of the needy poor.

Relief of suffering and rehabilitation goals have been given emphasis by social scientists in recent years: "In sum, social welfare may be characterized most accurately as an emerging institution whose core function is mutual support."[15] Zald underlines the primary welfare purpose of restoring or maintaining incapacitated "members of the society at a minimum level of personal and social functioning."[16] And Wilensky and Lebeaux have pointed up the benefits of the welfare system for the individual who can no longer properly function, rather than the benefits of the welfare system for the nonpoor.[17]

Yet the discussion of goals of many such analysts seems rather limited, in that it focuses on the positive benefits of an allegedly altruistic welfare system for the functioning of the poor. The use of welfare programs to maintain social order or reform the morals of the poor has been given much less attention. Peirce has suggested that many welfare analysts assume that "society, in creating and tolerating a social welfare system, is basically and largely motivated by charitable and altruistic purposes."[18] In recent years a few have emphasized the perhaps less obvious, and less often discussed, goals of welfare. In a broad argument about welfare states Miliband has argued that in recent decades the intervention of Western governments on behalf of those without property has been the "ransom" necessary to maintain the basic structure of economic inequality.[19] To a substantial degree, concessions in capitalist countries in the direction of such things as expanded social insurance and public assistance programs to benefit workers have come as the result of popular protest. In the United States this can be seen in the expansion of government welfare action in the 1930s, when rising unemployment and concomitant worker protest contributed to major decisions to channel money to those in distress. Historically, a cyclical expansion of public assistance arrangements has functioned to defuse outbreaks of revolts of the poor and "to mute civil disorder." [20] These first steps toward a welfare state, social insurance and public assistance, have been altered from time to time, but not always in the expansive direction. In the 1960s, with the rise of protest by a variety of dissident civil rights and welfare rights organizations, there was some relaxing of assistance restrictions (often the result of court decisions), but this has been followed in the 1970s by some moves to restrict assistance.

Regarding the goal of reinforcing work norms and maximizing the work effort of the poor, Cloward and Piven argue that once a political crisis is past, a capitalist government may retreat to a more restrictive posture in regard to welfare, to policies which insure even large numbers of low-wage workers for the relevant economic sectors.[21] In order to force the poor to take any available work, relief is cut back or hedged with eligibility and payment restrictions. Yet in the recent past governmental welfare restrictions have not always been immediate or across-the-board. Some welfare programs seem to be continued more or less unchanged as prophylactics against the possible resurgence of protest, even though others are reduced.

Moreover, all welfare programs in the United States have been hemmed in with work ethic restrictions. At all times the American welfare system has manifested a concern for the supply of low-wage workers; the goal of forcing the work activity or work seeking of the poor has seldom been forgotten even when welfare aid programs have been expanded somewhat. This has been quite evident in the slow development of state programs for unemployed male workers with families and the relatively low monetary payments for recipients. These actions clearly set limits as to the number of workers who can consider welfare in times of need. Thus it would seem that the governmental concern for defusing political protest and the objective of work reinforcement operate somewhat independently, both being reflected in the goals and consequences of welfare programs.

Other related purposes have been periodically reflected in welfare programs in the United States, including moral reformation and rehabilitation of the poor. The traditional concern with shaping the attitudes and morals of the poor goes back at least to the Protestant Reformation. This objective has been reflected at all levels in the American system, from Congress to local relief offices. As we will see shortly, recipients' sexual behavior and housekeeping patterns, to take two examples, have been the explicit focus of agency activities. Stimulating the motivation and ambition of the poor is an ancient concern. More recently, a purpose has been suggested for the welfare system which was not central in the past—that of rehabilitating the work skills of welfare recipients. Rehabilitation has been seen as encompassing social work services provided to recipients in order to make them more self-sufficient, including job counseling services and health care services. Yet in practice this relatively new concern with rehabilitation seems to blend together the older purposes of charity, moral reform, and maintenance of the existing economic order.

Of course, these goals are not mutually exclusive. Various assistance programs reflect elements of all of them. Moreover, some are more overt than others. Those objectives closely tied to the preservation of the existing order receive less publicity than those which reflect charitable aims. Day-in and day-out activities are enmeshed in an intricate bureaucratic complex, the members of which may be only dimly aware of the covert purposes. Analysis of the purposes and functions of welfare should go beyond this level of consciousness. "Any analysis of the social functions of the social welfare system must begin with the basic and overriding recognition that the system operates to maintain society essentially as it is." [22] In the section that follows, we hope to make clear the variety of manifest purposes and the sometimes hidden functions imbedded in the welfare system.

THE STRUCTURE OF PUBLIC
ASSISTANCE

Before we review some of the critical purposes that have been reflected in the actual operation of the contemporary welfare system, it will be useful to sketch out in a broad way certain important aspects or components of the public assistance system. Figure 1 offers a simplified diagram of these components.

FIGURE 1
THE PUBLIC ASSISTANCE SYSTEM
AND ITS ENVIRONMENT

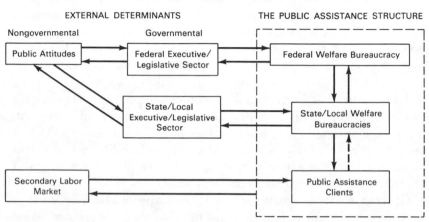

There are three major sectors to the public assistance system per se and a number of important external sectors that have a significant influence on the operation of that system.[23] Examination of the management sectors reveals a multitiered administrative setup with agencies at the federal, state, and local levels. The federal welfare bureaucracy has its own internal layers of organizational complexity; the major agencies at this level are in the Department of Health, Education and Welfare (HEW), although other federal agencies play a role in specific programs. Each state has had a department of public welfare that has traditionally shaped most of the assistance programs within its borders. The local agencies at municipal and county levels vary from state to state in degree of independence from state authority. Decisions often flow down from the top of this system, such as mandated changes in regulations. A decision (or indecision) at the state or local level can in turn have a significant effect on the federal bureaucracy. Regulations imposed by officials in Washington, D.C. shape the lives of administrators down the line, although state and local officials have often ignored these regulations or implemented them in a fashion congruent with local opinion. At a lower level in this hierarchy are the welfare workers in local agencies who actually administer the programs and provide the money and services.

Beneath the welfare hierarchy stand the recipients, those who have come to local welfare agencies for aid. Recipients have not been as well organized as the bureaucracies. Until recently, their position in the system was largely passive; they routinely absorbed the impact of decisions reached above. In the late 1960s, however, a few organizations of welfare recipients, such as the National Welfare Rights Organization, began to have an effect on administrative operations, primarily at the local level. This modest influence is indicated by the dotted line pointing upward in Figure 1.

Outside the public assistance system per se are a number of external determinants which greatly influence its shape and operation—the legislative (and executive) branches of federal, state, and local governments, the attitudes of the general public, and the secondary labor market. Of major importance are the legislatures. The U.S. Congress and the state legislatures control the major purse strings and thus the amount of money available for use at the various administrative levels. Thus actions taken by legislatures on the establishment and rules of welfare programs often have a dramatic impact on local welfare agencies. Historically, the executive branches (including the president and governors) have had less influence on the shape of welfare programs than federal and state (and local) legislative bodies, but periodically the officials there have played some role in developing new welfare programs, in abandoning old ones, or in imposing new restrictions on existing programs.

Another outside determinant of the welfare system is the secondary labor market, that part of the economy which provides most of the low-wage and irregular jobs that exist for unskilled workers. Enterprises in this secondary market employ on a short-term or irregular basis some adults who must in periods of unemployment or partial employment consider welfare as an alternative or supplementary source of income. Therefore unemployment trends in the secondary labor market area can affect the number and situation of the poor, many of whom move from low-wage jobs to welfare in times of job scarcity. Others are forced to supplement their low-wage jobs with meager welfare payments. Moreover, the requirements of the low-wage sector have tended to keep welfare payments low.

The impact average citizens have had on welfare programs seems to result primarily from constant reiteration of the ideology of individualism. Their attitudes toward the poor, particularly toward those poor requesting public aid, have historically been rather negative. We will examine these attitudes in some detail in the next chapter, but we can recall their importance here. The dogged persistence of negativism toward the poor has been one significant factor shaping legislative and executive restrictiveness in regard to welfare programs, payments, and regulations. Legislators and other elected officials at all levels of government have been influenced by prevailing views of the poor and of welfare recipients; they have in turn shaped the views of constituents on welfare in speeches and in policy-making activity. This relationship between public officials and prevailing public ideologies is even more direct, in that a majority of legislators seem to share the dominant negative view of the poor.

There are other organizations, such as the courts and social worker organizations, which periodically have affected the welfare system, but these do not seem to be quite as consistently important as the outside determinants just noted. Keeping these components in mind, we can now trace a few selected issues and historical events that illustrate the importance of goals and of social and administrative structure in the contemporary welfare system.

CONGRESS AND WELFARE

The contemporary public assistance system was inaugurated by the 1935 Social Security Act, which was the one major part of the New Deal relief "revolution" destined to survive. Yet even this modest step was taken against opposition. In spite of growing support from some groups of working-class Americans, there was extensive opposition from other influential groups. Local business and government officials expressed the fear that such legislation would destroy individual initiative, although some came to see this action as necessary to defuse protest. Supporters of private charity groups feared the political use of welfare and the lack of scrutiny of individual households.

From their beginning in the 1930s, assistance programs were carefully restricted in a number of important ways. Purposes other than relieving the suffering of the poor were clear in congressional discussion. An economic concern was evident. Southern legislators and other conservatives were concerned with protecting the low-wage structure of the South against generous welfare assistance levels and also with insuring that federal officials, who might be sympathetic to needy blacks, would have little to say about how assistance programs were operated. Such conservative opposition led to congressional rejection of more liberal assistance proposals, including one provision which would have allowed aid for all needy children and another which would have ensured greater federal supervision. Administration of new aid programs was to remain firmly in the hands of state and local officials. The wording of the final legislation was such as to allow the Southern states to protect their structure of racial inequality—that is, to discriminate on racial grounds in the paying of assistance.[24]

Moreover, resistance to public assistance in Congress was not as great as it might have been, because many assumed that assistance programs were temporary and residual programs designed to meet the current crisis and would wither away as social insurance programs began to take effect. Many viewed the welfare programs as a temporary liability for governments. As it turned out, this assumption was wrong. The view of welfare as temporary and residual soon began to give way in the face of the rising welfare rolls in the 1940s and 1950s. The former assumption was in line with conservative capitalistic thinking about workers, their families, and the allegedly laissez-faire economy. An institutional approach which viewed welfare as a normal first-line defensive institution was rare until the shift to government intervention to save capitalism in the 1930s. Industrialization and urbanization of the economy, as well as new political pressures tied to those social processes, had led to a shift away from an often ad hoc and primarily local public relief system to one that was built into the fabric of federal government.

In the decade of the 1930s, for the first time, major provisions for relief programs were built into federal law. Federal grants-in-aid were provided for the states (and localities) to help finance a sizable portion of costs under major assistance programs. A categorical approach was to be used, one that limited cash assistance to certain categories of the poor, a strategy which was similar to that of earlier state and local mother's aid programs. This approach was based on the assumption that relief had to be restricted and that the major reasons for poverty that should concern government were blindness, old age, and dependent motherhood. Consequently, the original welfare legislation provided fiscal aid for programs only for three groups among the poor: Aid to the Blind (AB), Old Age Assistance (OAA), and Aid to Dependent Children (ADC). By 1940 most state legislatures had responded to the congressional challenge by passing the necessary legislation to implement new programs or expand existing assistance programs; slowly, programs to use federal grants-in-aid were established in most states. Yet the number of recipients remained low until the 1940s.

Numerous modifications have been made in these programs by Congress since their inception. The major changes have included the establishment of a program of federal grants for Aid to the Permanently and Totally Disabled (APTD) in 1950. Major additions to the ADC (now called AFDC) program have included provisions for the payment of aid to two new groups among the poor: (1) adults caring for dependent children, added in 1950, and (2) needy children with unemployed parents (AFDC-U), added in 1961.[25] New groups of the poor, left out in the cold for decades, have slowly been added to the cash aid programs, although many of the poor have remained conspicuously absent in the categorical system. There has been substantial legislative reluctance in numerous states to take on some of the new categorical assistance programs; this reluctance often reflects the objectives of maintaining a supply of low-wage workers and of keeping state public aid expenditures low. Thus, as of 1970, half the states had no program of aid to families with unemployed fathers (AFDC-U), perhaps one of the most important programs for the poor. This reluctance, together with state administrative control over all assistance programs developed between the 1930s and the early 1970s, points up the basic philosophy of decentralization lying behind the structure of public assistance in the United States.

Federal financial involvement in welfare programs has grown steadily since the 1930s, including the federal share of public assistance costs. Major cash assistance programs have been supported in recent years substantially by federal funds. In addition to these federally funded programs, one other local welfare program termed General Assistance (GA) has been fostered by many state legislatures, but it is usually an extremely modest (short-term or emergency) aid program in which there is no federal financial involvement. These GA programs are a carryover from earlier, temporary local relief programs. Thus five basic programs—AB, AFDC, APTD, OAA, and GA—are the major direct-cash welfare programs for the poor in the United States. Other programs might conceivably be included here as involving aid for some of the poor (e.g., veteran's aid), but it is these direct-cash programs that most Americans have in mind when they discuss and criticize "welfare."

Congress has also authorized and funded a number of non-cash programs which are used to some degree not only by recipients of cash assistance but also by other poor persons not eligible for cash aid. These programs continue the in-kind aid which has characterized public action toward the Anglo-American poor for centuries. Inaugurated by Congress in a piecemeal fashion, important in-kind and service programs include food benefit programs, public housing, medical assistance programs, job-training programs, and a variety of social service programs. Most of these are recent innovations. Indeed, by the early 1970s some had not yet become available to cash-assistance recipients in many areas; and some may never be readily available to many recipients. Often the purpose of these in-kind measures has not been solely to benefit the welfare poor. Thus farmers have benefited substantially from the surplus commodities program; and some in-kind aid has been available to workers who cannot qualify for cash.

While our concern in this book is primarily with cash relief programs, a few notes on the more important in-kind programs will indicate the extent of the continuing and rather uneven federal involvement. One that has benefited many of the welfare poor is the surplus commodities program. Since the 1930s the federal government has distributed surplus food acquired under its price-support and surplus-removal operations. By 1940 the number receiving this in-kind aid had grown to nearly 12 million. The figure had declined significantly by the 1950s, but had risen to 6 million persons by the mid-1960s. Federal expenditures for this type of aid have fluctuated significantly, not only in relation to demand from the needy but also in relation to the supply of surplus food available. This is not a program strictly for welfare recipients; less than half of those aided in recent years have also been receiving cash assistance.[26] Another major program, "food stamps," provides discounts on most types of food for a growing number of the poor. Tried for a brief period in the 1930s, the program was started up again on a pilot basis in 1961; by the 1970s it had grown substantially. Food stamp participation rates for public assistance recipients have varied greatly. In 1971 the participation rates varied from 5 percent of AFDC recipients in Massachusetts to 83 percent in Washington.[27] In the early 1970s food stamp programs began to expand. As with other in-kind programs since the 1930s, these food benefit plans have aided very large numbers of those who are not public assistance recipients. And until very recently, many of the welfare poor had no access to such programs.

Another type of in-kind aid that has recently been made available by Congress to cash recipients is Medicaid. In 1960 a move was made in the direction of medical assistance for elderly welfare recipients; this program was soon replaced by a broader medical assistance program (MA) in the 1965 amendments to the Social Security Act. Adoption of this program by the state entails medical coverage for the four major categorical programs.[28] Certain non-welfare poor can be covered. Medicaid has received much critical comment and its original benefit and eligibility scope have been reduced.[29] Some states have been slow to participate or have significantly restricted eligibility.

Traditionally, welfare programs have been restricted by Congress and state legislatures, and implemented by administrative agencies, so that most poor Americans are not eligible or do not secure aid because of the stigma, preferring a low-paying job to public aid. By the early 1960s, a new concern with rehabilitating those on welfare had arisen in Congress. The underlying aim was not new, that of forcing self-support for recipients, but the means now encompassed "social services." In the 1950s amendments to the Social Security Act had noted that social services might be one way to move the poor from public aid to a rehabilitated status as working taxpayers, but no money was provided. In the first years of the John F. Kennedy administration prevention and rehabilitation became new bywords in discussing the "welfare problem." The 1962 amendments committed Congress and the rest of the federal government to supporting a broad range of state-controlled social services.[30] Congress initially committed itself to pay 75 percent of the cost of certain social services provided by the states to recipients. As a result there was a gradual expansion of services for welfare recipients, including moral, educational, health, and job counseling. Work programs, such as on-the-job training, could also be included. President Kennedy said: "I have approved a bill which makes possible the most far-reaching revision of our Public Welfare program since it was enacted in 1935." [31] He went on to emphasize that "our objective is to prevent or reduce dependency and to encourage self-care and self-support."

Many legislators and other public and private officials were enthusiastic about this "bold new approach" and saw it as a cure-all for an ailing system. Yet the hope that counseling and training programs would abolish the problem was not well-grounded. Increased social services failed to curtail growth. The expected miracle of reducing the cost or number of recipients did not happen. This should not have been surprising, since no one really knew just what services could do; they were untested. When the rehabilitation effort came along in the early 1960s, it unfortunately "tended to concentrate on ways to achieve long-run reductions in cost, although it has yet to be demonstrated either that there is any adequate substitute for money in relief or that money payments in relief have ever been adequate." [32]

Congress reacted strongly to the failure of social services to cure what was widely defined as the "welfare problem"; rising costs and caseloads triggered a severe reaction against welfare recipients, both in the states and in Congress. The 1967 Social Security amendments were quite different from those passed earlier. Vigorous attempts were made by Congress to freeze the growth of welfare rolls, particularly in AFDC. The first restriction was a freeze on federal grants to states, so that states could not without penalty increase the percentage of children receiving aid above the figure for that state as of January 1968. This forced many families to endure much suffering. "It's effect was to deny assistance to thousands of children who otherwise would have received it, to reduce the level of payments to those assisted, and to shift a part of the cost from the federal government to the states." [33] The opposition to this extreme restrictiveness was so extensive, in this decade of accelerating protest from dissident minorities and rising state costs resulting from these provisions, that Congress backed off and repealed the provision a few years later.

A second change imbedded in 1967 legislation was a get-tough provision that required the states to cut off welfare (AFDC) payments to any able-bodied person who refused to take any job or training offered.[34] Recipients who worked were allowed to keep a portion of earnings, up to a limit. A Work Incentive (WIN) program was established to provide job training and jobs for adult recipients, including mothers (a new emphasis); this program was to be operated by the Department of Labor. This WIN program soon revealed serious problems. AFDC fathers lost all benefits if they worked more than 100 hours in a month, regardless of low earnings. Additional income also reduced access to in-kind benefits. Up to 1971 the figures for successful completion of the WIN training program (on the job three months after placement) were less than 24,000 out of more than 2 million assessed recipients. More than 8 out of 10 of those assessed, however, were considered inappropriate for referral (because of illness, etc.) to job training by the agencies involved.[35] Perhaps most important, large numbers of those who had completed training were still awaiting placement because of the state of the economy and the other barriers of the primary labor market. A critical determinant of the success or failure of WIN and similar work training programs seems to be the character of the labor demand in local economy, the extent of unemployment, and employer attitudes to accepting trainees for better-paying jobs. Some analysts even regard training programs as primarily temporary sources of income for the poor, because employers of skilled persons will "for the most part, simply not hire the poor, regardless of the quality of the training they acquire, while secondary employers—having no choice, and no pressing need for skilled labor—will hire them whether they have had training or not." [36] At best, training programs have apparently recirculated a few trained recipients back into the lowest-paying sector of the economy.

One of the ironies of the 1967 amendments is that they dramatically increased federal welfare expenditures in social services because of an additional congressional provision. Preoccupied with restricting the poor and wishing to encourage some expansion of services, Congress allowed the states to increase the amount of federal aid for current social services. As a result, in the next few years administrators broadly defined social services, to the extent of including services to persons who were not welfare recipients. In addition, services could be purchased by state agencies from other private or public agencies, which resulted in an escalation of expenditures. It is not clear just how much of this money actually benefited welfare recipients. Total federal subsidies for state social service expenditures escalated from $248 million in 1967 to a projected figure of several billion in fiscal 1973. Not surprisingly, a number of attempts were made to limit spending for so-called services. In 1972 a cap of $2.5 billion was placed on social service expenditures for fiscal 1973, and limitations were placed on the proportion of expenditures that could be made for non-welfare recipients.[37] This latter provision had turned out to be a type of revenue sharing by which hard-pressed state governments used a loophole to buttress their own shaky fiscal foundations.

The late 1960s and early 1970s have seen increased congressional action in regard not only to work relief and work motivation but also to a range of other moral reformation issues as well. Concern for the morality of the poor continues to preoccupy numerous congressional analysts; topics such as child support and paternity have recently grabbed congressional attention. Although most states have civil and criminal penalties for fathers who do not provide for their welfare and non-welfare children, studies have shown that thousands of warrants have not been served. Such data has incensed certain congressmen. Thus the House Ways and Means Committee and the Senate Finance Committee have tried to develop and implement solutions to the child support problem. Proposals for a nationwide parent locator service, for laboratories to establish paternity, and for the garnishment of wages of absent fathers in welfare and non-welfare families have been forthcoming. In addition, a number of actions have been specifically focused on welfare families. These have included proposals making nonsupport by a welfare parent a criminal offense, giving the U.S. attorney general responsibility over notification procedures in connection with desertion cases, and requiring mothers as a condition of receiving aid to cooperate in locating the absent father. Other proposals (in proposed 1972 legislation) included federal enforcement of support payments to welfare mothers, as well as the exemption of a portion of support income from consideration for welfare purposes.[38] Though these provisions have not yet been put into effect (as of mid-1974), it is likely that even if they were implemented they would further oppress the poor without reducing the number of children on the rolls. One study of absent fathers of welfare children revealed that of those whose incomes were known, half had no significant income and most of the rest had incomes of less than $400 a month.[39] Requiring support payments of such low-income fathers as a major way of solving welfare problems would seem a rather ineffective approach. Even more important, perhaps, is the discrimination against welfare families imbedded in much of this proposed legislation. Much more stringent action is suggested for welfare families than for non-welfare families with similar problems. While some of this activity indicates a concern for welfare costs, the specter of moral reform still seems to haunt the congressional stage.

THE PRESIDENCY AND WELFARE

Over the last few decades, as the preceding discussion suggests, presidents have generally been less influential than the Congress in shaping public assistance. In his tardy response to growing protest in the 1930s President Franklin D. Roosevelt was instrumental in setting up the Committee on Economic Security which drew up the Social Security Bill and its welfare provisions. Yet these public assistance provisions were carefully worked over by Congress, which put its ideological imprint on the final draft. From time to time, Presidents Harry Truman and Dwight D. Eisenhower commented on the welfare system, occasionally becoming involved in issues such as the federal-state share of costs, but neither had much of a lasting impact on the system.[40] Under President John F. Kennedy, there was successful presidential activity in the direction of expanding social services. Yet it was the Congress that ultimately shaped the legislation; and it was Congress that pressed for increases in federal sharing of expenditures for the adult categories, not the Kennedy Administration. President Lyndon B. Johnson gave relatively little attention to welfare, although he took extensive action in regard to the poor, particularly in his War on Poverty programs. HEW Secretary John Gardner, more or less on his own, did succeed in the reorganization of the federal welfare administration, to some extent separating the administration of payments from that of social services; state agencies were pressured to separate payments and services. Congress played the major role in pressing for changes in welfare in the Johnson years.

Indeed, welfare administrators have traditionally been closer to Congress than to presidents. Since Roosevelt, there has been relatively little presidential attention devoted to welfare, beyond the standard rhetorical comments on "holding the line" in presidential addresses. With the exception of Kennedy's influence on social services legislation and President Richard M. Nixon's abortive thrust at a Family Assistance Plan (FAP), a proposal we will deal with in a later chapter, there appears to have been a significant lack of leadership or influence on specific welfare issues at the presidential level, a political situation which has operated to reinforce welfare localism.

WELFARE LOCALISM

One of the traditional distinguishing characteristics of the welfare system in the United States is the power of state and local welfare bureaucracies, buttressed by the power of state legislatures and legislative committees, which have together been more influential than the federal bureaucracy in shaping many critical aspects of welfare. Indeed, public assistance has not been a uniform national operation, but rather fifty different operations with considerable variability.

Welfare localism was built into contemporary public assistance programs by a Depression Congress strongly oriented to states' rights. Federal grants-in-aid were seen primarily as back-up support for state and local agencies unable to meet the needs of the destitute. Because at the outset federal support was expected to be a relatively short-term operation, maximum state and local authority seemed natural. Numerous provisions of the draft Social Security Bill were revised or cut out to maximize local control, and substantial variation in payment levels was permitted. "It is indicative of the degree of freedom first accorded the states by the public assistance titles of the Social Security Act that Congress did not see fit to authorize denial of federal aid to a state that established substandard benefits." [41]

Why did this emphasis on management of welfare below the federal level come to dominate in the years between 1940 and 1970? The answer to this question seems to lie in part in the American tradition of federalism, taken in the sense of the determination to maximize local control and in the tendency to regard the welfare poor as lazy reprobates or deviants in need of close supervision and moral reformation. The emphasis on control of the poor at the local level is one of the important examples of decentralization and of cooperation between federal and local levels of government. [42] Traditionally, as we saw in Chapter 2, the emphasis on strong local control in welfare programs has been coupled with an ideology of individualism emphasizing the immoral character of the poor. Historically, the control of alleged deviance has been left to local agencies, a tendency evident in the early English Poor Laws. Of course, poor relief programs in the United States stressed local responsibility well before the new legislation of the 1930s. Since then, moreover, state and local governments have persistently tried to maximize their own administrative control, even while they were forced to seek and receive expanded federal financial assistance, as well as to accept new federal supervision of their administrative procedures and eligibility rules. The new welfare legislation of the 1930s, generated initially to support bankrupt state and local relief agencies, fostered a substantial expansion in states and localities of federally supported welfare programs. The stage was set, clearly, for conflict between advocates of federal and local administrative control.

This delegation to the states of substantial control over the implementation and administration of federally financed welfare programs was dramatized in the existence of corruption and mismanagement in some states, which in turn led to greater federal intervention and supervision of state and local administrative procedures. The first heat that seared the new public assistance programs emanated from political scandals. The Social Security Board, the original supervisory agency, withdrew federal funds from state administrations in Oklahoma and Ohio because of the use of welfare rolls for political purposes.[43] By the 1940s the federal welfare agency was forced to expand surveillance of state and local programs.

Public interest in welfare aid had grown somewhat by the late 1940s. Even in the late 1940s and early 1950s a few investigations were conducted into public assistance by state and municipal agencies. These investigations reflected public concern with the growth of the rolls in a time of prosperity (a concern that would be much greater in the 1960s). Attacks on the confidentiality of welfare records surfaced in a few states, perhaps a concrete result of growing public acceptance of undocumented stereotypes of welfare recipients. Officials in Indiana and in a number of other states urged disclosure of records. As a result of pressure from state governors and other officials, Congress passed the Jenner amendment permitting public disclosure by state agencies of those on state relief rolls, within certain limits.[44] This was an important example of state pressure leading to federal welfare action.

Under federal law each state desiring federal aid is required to draw up an approved "plan," a nonenforceable statement of program arrangements which is basically a promise made to the federal government as the basis for a contract for federal financial assistance. Federal regulations have provided rather broad limits for state and local plans and for welfare administration. Requirements include "stipulations that the plan must be Statewide in character, that it be operated by a single agency with State financial participation, and that the machinery for appeals exists." [45] Under federal law and administrative regulations applicants must be examined for need. Certain eligibility criteria, such as age, have been specified at the federal level. The costs of welfare programs have been divided between federal, state, and local governments, with the federal percentage sizable but variable from one program to the next. The Department of Health, Education and Welfare is ultimately responsible for supervising state plans and administrative programs. Moreover, from the inception of welfare programs in the 1930s, state legislatures and welfare agencies have had considerable *discretion* in determining the administrative organization and extent of programs, the level of cash payments, and a number of the eligibility criteria. Administrative organization also varies by state. In some states programs have been administered by local arms of state agencies; in others, separate local agencies have substantial authority and are supervised by state agencies.[46]

Nowhere is state discretion more evident than in decisions to participate in programs and to set payment levels. This can be seen in the fact that as of 1970 half the states had not begun the AFDC-U program authorized by Congress. State agencies have also had significant control over payments. They have established their own minimum standards of subsistence for recipients, with considerable variation in items included. They have often paid only a percentage of this minimum level of subsistence to recipients. In the late 1960s twenty-six states were found to be making payments below their own minimum cost standards in AFDC programs and sixteen in OAA programs.[47] One reason for this was the legislated ceiling or closed-end appropriation governing state relief expenditures in all states, a restriction that can force reductions in payments as the number of recipients increases.[48]

Low and variable payments have characterized state and local programs from the beginning. Although Massachusetts averaged $61.07 (per month) for its assistance payments to ADC families late in 1939, Arkansas averaged only $8.10.[49] More recently, in June 1971 *average* monthly cash payments to AFDC families reportedly ranged from a low of $52 in Mississippi to $266 in Hawaii. The United States average was $183 a month. APTD payments averaged only $98 per recipient in the same month, ranging from a low of $52 in Alabama to a high of $174 in Alaska. AB payments averaged only $104, with a low of $66 in Mississippi and a high of $175 in Alaska. OAA payments averaged $76, ranging from $49 in South Carolina to $165 in New Hampshire. As can be seen from the national averages, monthly payments in each category have made it likely that an *average* welfare family or individual would be at or below the federal government's own poverty line, which is very low. These low payments are an indication of the use of welfare rolls to restrict the poor and to insure maximum work effort, no matter what the personal or family cost may be.[50]

In addition, no group of recipients of government subsidies has had to endure such a lengthy list of eligibility and other restrictions as have welfare recipients (particularly AFDC recipients). The congressional legislation setting up public assistance allowed states to develop their own income and property restrictions and noneconomic restrictions as well. "Long-time residence in the area, adherence to established standards of moral conduct, and a willingness to trade in certain personal liberties are among the common formal and informal noneconomic factors that go to make eligibility in many jurisdictions." [51] The fundamental goals of moral reformation and social control were evident in restrictions which were seldom challenged until the 1960s.

Over the last few decades, as has been mentioned before, numerous states have attempted to purge their rolls of "immoral" recipients, to tighten restrictions so that only "moral" recipients remain on the rolls. This has sometimes been done by means of a so-called "suitable home" requirement, applied to mothers with dependent children. The presence of illegitimate children or a casual acquaintance with a man (or rumors to that effect) have been used as reasons for removing families. "Suitable home" provisions have resulted in removing a disproportionate number of black and other nonwhite children from the welfare rolls.[52] These provisions were not spelled out by federal law, but soon after the enactment of the Social Security Act many states adopted this critical restriction. By 1941 a majority of the states had some type of "suitable home" provision; and by the mid-1940s states were encouraged to repeal this provision, but while fifteen did so, five more adopted it! After World War II the growth in the rolls and in attacks on public assistance meant that the "restrictive welfare policies became increasingly viable devices for applying social and economic sanctions against misbehaving, nonconforming, and impoverished parents and their children." [53] By 1960 almost half the states still had this provision.

In a notorious 1960 case Louisiana authorities removed more than 22,000 children in 6,000 families (almost all were black) from its rolls as part of a state investigation into "suitable homes." [54] In most cases this meant that there were some illegitimate children in the families. The reaction of HEW and the Social Security Administration to this state action aimed primarily against black recipients was slow; action against Louisiana was effectively delayed. A 1961 HEW ruling limited the application of the "suitable home" provision and resulted in changes in the rule in a number of states. Then the 1962 Social Security amendments provided that a state with a "suitable home" requirement would not lose federal aid if the children involved were otherwise provided for. The state of Louisiana had in effect won, because no federal money had been withheld for noncompliance. Although Louisiana authorities had to support these needy children, they soon adopted other strategies to reduce the number of AFDC families.[55] Not until the 1960s were "suitable home" requirements challenged and disallowed. But other actions have been directed toward close supervision of the marital lives of recipients. In 1950 Congress, in response to state pressure, adopted the Noleo amendment to the Social Security Act.[56] This amendment made public aid contingent on the mother's cooperation in locating a deserting father; it required that enforcement officials be notified of desertions.

Surprise searches have been used in attempts to find illegitimate objects or activities for persons in all categories; but indiscriminate raids and unannounced visits have been used most often in attempts to ferret out the lovers of welfare mothers. By the "man-in-the-house" rule those who are found with men are cut off the rolls on the grounds that the man is a substitute parent. AFDC mothers have been forced to accept uninvited visits and searches by caseworkers from welfare agencies, an eligibility condition which has for many years violated the civil liberties of clients. At least one lawyer as early as 1963 questioned whether these unannounced searches were constitutional, urging that they were violations of the fourth and fourteenth amendments.[57] Yet until the late 1960s there seemed to be little federal or state government concern with the fact that this type of search was a common practice of local welfare agencies. Indeed, surveillance was encouraged.

Not only have welfare agencies often watched over the marital and sex lives of recipients, but they have supervised other aspects of their lives. "Caseworkers may go uninvited into their homes to scrutinize their housekeeping methods and their child-rearing practices."[58] Another example of state interference in the lives of recipients has been in the form of extreme birth control pressure. In the early 1970s a number of news stories probed the fact that local welfare boards had participated in the forced sterilization of welfare mothers.[59]

Until a Supreme Court decision in the late 1960s, another sacrifice that was demanded of assistance clients was embodied in residency requirements: Residence requirements, five years for adult programs and one year for ADC (the permitted maximum), were established in most participating states soon after welfare programs were inaugurated in the 1930s. Congressional reluctance to change the maximum requirements was tied to respect for states' rights. The welfare stereotype underlying the views of opponents of relaxing residency requirements has been suggested by Steiner:

Supporters of residence requirements do not want the needy flitting around in hopes of bettering their income or getting more sunshine. And on this latter point, there is more firmness than on any of the other noneconomic eligibility conditions. Poor people are expected to stay put.[60]

This view of the poor has been closely tied to concern with a regulated low-wage work force and the maintenance of economic order. As we have seen in a previous chapter, this dates back many centuries in Anglo-American history.

PYRAMIDING ELIGIBILITY RESTRICTIONS: THE NEWBURGH FIASCO

Perhaps the most famous local attempt to expand these eligibility restrictions even further occurred in Newburgh, New York in the early 1960s. As was mentioned in Chapter 1, an extreme attempt was made there to maximize control over the morality and work effort of the poor. Local and national concern with welfare "bums," "cheats," and "chiselers" was pervasive when in 1961 Newburgh's city manager publicly criticized recipients and attempted to catch chiselers by ordering all recipients to pick up checks at the police department—none, incidentally, were discovered.[61]

Later the local government set up thirteen additional eligibility conditions for aid, designed to cut back the number of recipients. These included requirements that applicants new to the city show a concrete offer of employment, that those who voluntarily left jobs for any reason be denied relief, that voucher payments be substituted for cash relief, and that AFDC aid be limited to three months. A "suitable home" provision was established. The state welfare department conducted a hearing on the restrictions, during which time the city manager became a national hero. Many prominent officials spoke or wrote in support of the strict Newburgh controls. Mail from all parts of the country poured in supporting the effort to maximize the control of the welfare poor. One setback came when a careful combing for able-bodied men to throw off the rolls turned up *one* possible case. Eventually, the New York State Welfare Board ordered Newburgh officials not to implement their new code; and eventually the Supreme Court issued an injunction. Subsequently, all but one of the restrictions were found to be illegal.[62]

Nonetheless, the impact of this punitive attack on welfare clients continued long after it was legally stopped. Newspapers carried stories of new control actions by public officials around the nation. The defense of Newburgh recipients and the exploding of the welfare myths came too late to affect public opinion. Newburgh had become a symbol of maintaining social order and middle-class morality by a stepped-up campaign of punitive action against recipients.[63] Nor was Newburgh an isolated case; similar punitive attempts have been made in other areas in the last decade.

NONCOMPLIANCE

Among the most important indicators of the strength of traditional state and local control are many reported examples of noncompliance with federal law and administrative regulations. Recent pressure from welfare rights organizations led to a report by HEW indicating that at least thirty-nine states were at the beginning of the 1970s violating federal administrative regulations or laws. Some violations were quite serious, including the failure of numerous states to abolish eligibility requirements no longer permitted by the courts.[64]

The failure of state welfare agencies to comply with federal regulations has often meant that clients have not received the aid or treatment to which they were legally entitled. A number of state agencies have been slow to comply with new regulations or laws requiring state cost standard increases in the form of cost-of-living adjustments and protection of recipient rights by means of procedural safeguards. Although most evidence on noncompliance appears to be recent, it is probable that many state and local agencies have ignored completely, or implemented reluctantly, numerous laws and administrative regulations.[65]

A basic reason for these violations seems to lie in HEW's lax enforcement. This has resulted in part from the cumbersome regulations and remedial procedures available and in part from a lack of enforcement staff. Until recently, the lack of client protest has also been important. Perhaps the most important factor has been the power of local and state agencies. Evidence has accumulated in recent years indicating that HEW did not know much about particular administrative operations at the local level or intentionally preferred to exert only modest control. "HEW, in most situations, reflects the views of state agencies and they, in turn, wield enormous power in the administration of welfare." [66] Also important are judicial and political considerations. Courts have until recently emphasized the importance of state, over federal, laws and discretion; thus many defiant state officials have felt that they would not be disciplined for failure to comply with federal law because of friends in Congress and the White House; this has been particularly true when a state administration was of the same political party as the presidential administration.[67] Thus the inability or reluctance of HEW officials to *enforce* regulations against state bureaucracies has been a major reason for noncompliance. Indeed, until the 1970s there were virtually no court cases challenging state noncompliance.

THE COURTS AND THE STATES

One governmental sector that has only recently begun to have a major effect on the welfare system is the federal (and, to a lesser extent, the state) court system. The rise of civil rights and welfare rights activity and organization in the 1960s led, directly and indirectly, to a series of court cases that challenged not only eligibility restrictions but also the failure of states to comply with new laws or regulations. Important examples of court attempts to deal with state noncompliance have come from California.[68] Two cases there involved payment levels. In one case California did not conform for nearly two years to a new statute requiring cost-of-living raises in AFDC need standards and maximum payments. The change only came with a struggle involving federal courts, state courts, HEW, and welfare rights groups. In a second case California welfare departments reportedly violated federal and state laws in denying recipients a 1967 federally mandated work incentive (income disregard). "As a result, some 28,000 families in California were illegally deprived of an average $28 per month in welfare payments for at least 14 months." [69] Relief was again sought and attained in the state courts. Two additional California cases involved the rights of relief recipients in regard to termination and hearings. Sitkin has summarized them as follows:

(a) Federal law required California to provide recipients with notice and hearing before their benefits were terminated or reduced, but California failed to meet those requirements. Its failure and resulting administrative chaos cost the taxpayers of California millions of dollars.

(b) Federal law required an administrative fair hearing decision to be rendered within 60 days of the request, but California took 6 months or more to render its decisions.[70]

In both cases relief in the state and federal courts was sought and attained.

Yet these violations of hearing and notice laws and regulations by the state of California were not unique. Other states have also been guilty of this type of noncompliance as well. Even the Supreme Court has become involved. In two important cases, Goldberg v. Kelly (1970) and Wheeler v. Montgomery (1970), the Supreme Court ruled that a fair evidentiary hearing and proper notice must be given a welfare recipient before payments can be stopped. California was involved in the Wheeler case. These cases were milestones in the fight by recipients and their sympathizers to force states to comply with federal laws and regulations that ostensibly protected their rights.

Since 1968, under pressure from welfare recipient groups and civil rights organizations, the federal courts have slowly begun to deal with restrictive eligibility requirements. Lower federal courts have handed down some important decisions. The state of Georgia's "employable mother" rule was successfully challenged in federal courts on the grounds that it was used primarily to keep black mothers off the rolls.[71] Noneconomic restrictions have also been challenged at the Supreme Court level. Thus an important 1968 decision, King v. Smith, knocked down the "man-in-the-house" rule in Alabama—which affected at least eighteen other states and the District of Columbia as well. Another decision, Shapiro v. Thompson (1969), rejected minimum residence requirements as violating the Constitution, thus expanding welfare programs somewhat to include a modest number of recent migrants in at least forty states. In 1971 decisions the Supreme Court ruled against a state's prohibition of relief to resident aliens, a decision that affected minority residents in a number of states.[72] Not surprisingly, the knocking down of restrictions intended to keep the rolls lean has contributed to a growth in the number of recipients. Indeed, this elimination of some regulations by the Supreme Court in the 1960s lends support to those who argue that welfare programs have been used by governments to defuse protest during troubled times.

However, a new, if inconsistent, restrictiveness in Supreme Court decisions became evident as early as 1970. With the change in court perspective associated with the terms of President Richard M. Nixon came more decisions favorable to state restrictions on payments, as well as to state eligibility rules. In one case New York was permitted to pay less in benefits than its own established need level. In Dandridge v. Williams (1970) the Supreme Court ruled that Maryland's rather low payment ceiling was permissible, even though it was less than the officially determined need standard for poor welfare recipients. In Jefferson v. Hackney (1972) the court upheld the legality of reduced-cost standards and refused to knock down state discrimination in payment levels between "adult" and AFDC recipients. In Wyman v. James (1971) the Court upheld those local agencies that used periodic home visits by caseworkers to maintain surveillance of recipients and that terminated aid to recipients who refused this entry. State control was far from dead.

RECENT CHANGES IN WELFARE ADMINISTRATION

Within the last year (1973–1974) there have been some signs that the traditional imbalance of power that existed between federal and state governments in the welfare area may be shifting in the direction of increased federal administrative control. Federal fiscal and administrative involvement in the so-called "adult" programs (AB, APTD, OAA) has recently changed.

A Supplemental Security Income (SSI) program was approved by Congress and took effect in January 1974. It provides for a *federally administered* program for those currently eligible for the old OAA, APTD, and AB programs. The disabled, aged, and the blind may be able now to move out, to some degree, from under the stigma of "the dole." This program in effect sets minimum payment levels for assistance to those categories, a step that will raise payment levels in some states, and requires the same eligibility standards nationwide. Though the SSI program is federally administered in regard to basic payments and eligibility, the states have retained significant administrative control over nonfinancial services. Medicaid responsibilities, except for eligibility determination in some states, still belong to state and local agencies. State responsibility also holds for social services for adult clients and for Medicaid for formerly ineligible recipients. Most importantly, the federal SSI grant is a *minimum* payment which must be supplemented from state funds in many states. Supplements are administered through the federal agency in numerous states, but some states retain administrative control.[73] All these contingencies pose serious problems for the implementation and expansion of the SSI program, but expanded federal-state cooperation will probably be the ultimate result.

Whether this modest step toward federalization will be followed by more extensive federal involvement in the major AFDC programs remains to be seen. The resistance demonstrated by states' rights advocates in stopping President Nixon's innovative Family Assistance Plan (see Chapter 5), and, to a lesser extent, in keeping federalization steps limited to adult categories bodes ill for those who wish further federalization of welfare. The argument for a federally administered setup for AFDC usually stresses the tremendous variability in AFDC payments from state to state and the inability of the federal government to control the complex bureaucracy below. Perhaps more important is the serious financial difficulty in which many state welfare agencies still find themselves, resulting from inadequate tax resources in many state and local areas. Indeed, federalization of AFDC seems less likely than its replacement by some new income maintenance program. Such a step would clearly signal that the fiscal difficulties of states have led to a decline in "states' rights" and "local control" issues.

WELFARE RIGHTS: A RECENT TREND

At the bottom of the assistance system in Figure 1 (p. 56) stand the recipients, those among the poor who have come to local bureaucracies for aid. This lowly position is more than diagrammatic. Historically, public assistance recipients have not been as well organized as other welfare sectors. Until recently, their position was largely passive; this was the price they paid for public dependency. To take one important example, little in government manuals on welfare has related to grievance procedures for recipients upset with decisions made in their regard. Although many groups and individuals receiving federal subsidies have traditionally had a significant impact on legislative and executive decisions affecting their grants, welfare recipients have not been included in that group.

The lack of organizational activity among welfare recipients in the past is not surprising, given their lack of organizational experience, their already hard-pressed lives, and the fear of losing support payments. Before the burst of welfare rights activity in the 1960s the most successful recipient organizations had been among the needy aged in California. Pressuring Congress for new and expanded benefits, OAA-oriented California groups did contribute to improvements in aid, but successes were limited primarily to that state. To a lesser extent, the National Federation for the Blind had some effect on aid for the blind.[74] On the whole, little organizational activity was the rule among assistance recipients until the 1960s.

In the mid-1960s the AFDC-dominated National Welfare Rights Organization (NWRO) was formed as a consolidation of autonomous local welfare rights organizations formed a few years earlier. Many local organizations had grown up under the auspices of local War-on-Poverty or civil rights activities. In 1967 at a Commission on Civil Rights hearing in Mississippi, recipients (represented by NWRO) complained that they were not receiving the grants due them and that eligible families had been denied aid arbitrarily. Harsh local treatment in Mississippi became geographically clear in the testimony of those predominantly black recipients. This protest meeting was a clear indication that those at the bottom of the welfare system would no longer remain silent. Organizing activity accelerated in many states. The expanding protest of dissident nonwhite minorities in the 1960s had spilled over to welfare matters, and the growing number of welfare recipients meant a larger constituency. Marches by recipients in dozens of cities from Los Angeles to Washington and Boston demonstrated against the degradation of "the welfare." [75] Many were arrested for their protest efforts. Support, financial and otherwise, came from the welfare poor and from some liberals among the nonpoor.

What have these new organizations accomplished? Along with other organizations oriented to the poor, NWRO chapters have prepared manuals showing people how to secure maximum legal benefits and how to deal with illegal rejections. Consequently, numerous recipients have become well-informed about laws and regulations. In addition, in recent years some NWRO chapters have had some influence on acceptance and termination procedures affecting recipients. [76] Welfare rights activities have also led in a few cases to local benefit increases. One in-depth study of welfare rights activity in New York City came to the following conclusions:

In short, welfare rights groups emerge from our study as highly effective organizations during the period we studied. They were able to provide their membership with higher grant levels. This was a major benefit to the membership that, while it lasted, helped to ensure its commitment to the movement. At the same time, these organizations helped to bring many eligible non-recipients into the system by encouraging new applicants. This was, however, a by-product of their activities that did not benefit directly the membership. In other words, welfare rights activities provided a social good by assisting a larger percentage of families to obtain public assistance who were eligible for it under the law. [77]

Low-income families were here acting in their own economic self-interest. Unfortunately, in some areas such as New York City, the newly won grant increases were so troublesome to welfare agencies and state legislatures that certain types of aid (such as special allowances) were terminated. This impact has been an unintended side effect of organizing and protest activities. In addition, the greater knowledge about welfare among recipients as a result of rights groups' activity has had an impact, direct and indirect, on the growth of welfare rolls in some metropolitan areas.

Even broader effects should be noted. By the late 1960s welfare commissioners in a few states had begun to emphasize publicly the *eligible* people *not* on the welfare rolls, rather than the number of ineligible people on the rolls. Another main effect of welfare rights organizations has been a greater sense of efficacy among organized recipients.[78] This has manifested itself in recipients running for political office and expanding their activities in school organizations and at political conventions.

Gradually, the targets of welfare rights activities changed somewhat from strictly local matters to national problems, a change welcomed more by liberal allies than by recipients themselves. Yet welfare rights organizations have not as yet had much impact on Congress or on the executive branch. One exception to this statement was the modest role of NWRO in the axing of President Nixon's Family Assistance Program. Nor were they successful in getting NWRO's own version of a guaranteed annual income passed by the Congress. And over NWRO's insistent protests, the 1967 Social Security amendments were passed. Most of the impact of welfare rights activity has come at the local level, where fear of disorder has sparked some bureaucratic reaction. A main strategy has been one of creating inconveniences until some changes are made, as in this New York example:

The protest activity in New York, directed toward the achievement of higher cash benefit payments as its specific, immediate, and practical objective, uses welfare clients to inconvenience important parts of the community; plays upon the guilt felt by the city's enlightened political leaders as they are visibly confronted with visibly needy children; and frightens the city's middle class into believing that the welfare issue can endanger the peace of the city.[79]

Such tactics again suggest that expansion of welfare has occasionally been used to defuse protest. Currently, welfare rights organizations have declined somewhat in influence, probably because of funding difficulties and the recent loss of NWRO's charismatic leader, Dr. George A. Wiley. The economic base of local groups and NWRO has always been fragile. Since the late 1960s numerous groups have declined in strength or wavered on the brink of bankruptcy, and tax challenges from the Internal Revenue Service have made life very difficult for NWRO. Recently, an interesting shift in the tactics of NWRO can be seen in the attempt to build local groups around the 1974 Supplemental Security Income program.[80] NWRO has suggested that local welfare rights groups should establish SSI committees to gather information and hold workshops for interested people in the community. Aid to possible and actual SSI recipients by local welfare rights groups is recommended, as well as recruiting SSI recipients as members. This shift signals a new attempt to broaden the base of the welfare rights movement beyond its current dependence on AFDC recipients to the categories of aged, blind, and disabled. Whether or not this will reinvigorate the movement is an open question.

THE SECONDARY LABOR MARKET

An important outside sector affecting some aspects of the welfare system is the "secondary labor market," that part of the economy providing low-paid jobs for unskilled workers. This is a new topic in economic research, but is a suggestive conceptual development. The economy can be viewed as divided into two major sectors, the "core" and the "periphery." [81] Central to the core of the economy is the primary labor market, characterized by high productivity, high wages, highly profitable firms, a stable work force, and significant internal mobility chances for workers. The primary labor market is composed primarily of white and relatively affluent workers. The peripheral sector of the economy can be divided into several important subsectors; the secondary labor market is probably the most important of these. This labor market is typically characterized by relatively low productivity, low wages, modest profit firms with low market power, an unstable work force, and a scarcity of internal mobility chances. This market can also be seen as encompassing low-paying service-type jobs. This is a large labor market heavily populated by unskilled and minority workers.

The importance of this institutionalized and persisting division between skilled and unskilled workers is more than economic, for it is intimately related to prevailing work ideologies. Between 1870 and 1970 the American economy changed from a manufacturing-oriented capitalism to "monopoly capitalism," a stage with "enormous concentrations of economic power and huge corporate units of production." [82] The rise of unions and the socialist movement, coupled with periodic depressions, has posed a serious threat to capitalist organization. What has forestalled the development of working-class consciousness? One important strategy has been to minimize the extent to which skilled and unskilled workers could feel a kindred with one another by accentuating the status differences and rewards available to skilled workers. The segregation of workers in the dual labor market, and within primary firms as well, effectively accomplished this goal. Secondary jobs could be reserved for women, nonwhites, and young people with no fear that secondary groups would identify with primary groups. [83] Credentials, job titles, and variations in pay and privileges accentuate this stratification, which is further buttressed by the constant reinforcement of the attitudes previously termed ideology of individualism. Moreover, some have argued that the development of a much-criticized welfare system has diverted the attention of the poor from more radical demands and the attention, by means of an anti-welfare ideology, of the working and middle classes from their own inequality to the depressed poor, further reinforcing the segregation of workers. [84]

A few important alternatives to low-wage jobs in the unpredictable—and often high in unemployment—secondary market exist for poor workers. One area about which little is known is the "hustle" or crime economy. Alternatively, those who cannot find jobs can sometimes find a manpower training program which pays a small stipend and temporarily keeps them "employed."

Perhaps the most widely debated alternative to the secondary market is the "welfare economy," a sector reserved mainly to persons with various physical and skill disabilities. Thus the number of able-bodied, unemployed fathers who have access to welfare aid remains a small minority of all recipients. Although the image of the typical welfare recipient is of a lazy, nonwork-oriented person who is in a chronic condition of dependency passed on from generation to generation, the actual picture of a typical recipient is similar to that of workers with irregular or difficult work histories in the secondary labor market. For a number of the poor the relationship between the secondary labor market and welfare seems intimate. Enterprises and employers in the secondary market employ, often on a short-term basis, many adults with families who must in slack periods, or because of situational problems, consider welfare as an alternative to crime or starvation. Unskilled mothers separated from unskilled male workers forced to roam in an attempt to find secondary work can fall back on public assistance. Unemployment trends in the secondary area can affect the number and situation of the poor, many of whom move from low-wage jobs to welfare and back.

The sudden imposition of more restrictive welfare regulations can in turn significantly increase the pressure on the secondary labor market by forcing larger numbers of the disabled poor to compete for a limited number of low-paying jobs. Most welfare mothers have irregular or part-time work histories, but have worked in the secondary labor market for relatively low wages. Indeed, welfare sometimes supplements their wages while they are working. Particularly in the South, welfare aid has been used to keep unskilled workers, such as black field hands, supported between the picking seasons.[85] The character of demand in the secondary labor market has affected both state and federal government action in regard to expanding low welfare benefits to a subsistence level.

In addition, some officials have worried openly that even mildly improved welfare payments or fringe benefits will reduce the willingness of the very poor to do the dirty work of the society: the stoop farm labor, the ditch-digging, the maid services, the sanitation work.[86] They feel that benefits must be kept relatively low, so that some workers will be willing to do the society's low-paying dirty work. Changes in benefit levels can be a real problem in an economy with a low minimum wage.

CONCLUSION

In this chapter we have examined public subsidies and a number of external systems or sectors that have had an impact on one major type of public subsidy—welfare. We have not exhausted the list of external determinants of the American welfare system; some have barely been touched. One such factor is the prevailing ideology of individualism which will be examined in more detail in the next chapter. Another is the business community in general. Not only have secondary market employers and their friends in government had an important impact on unskilled workers, and on the public assistance system, but the business sector as a whole has set limits on welfare programs. At the federal level, lobbying from this sector has sometimes slowed the development of federal programs or spending in the welfare area. During the Great Depression business was a major source of opposition to New Deal legislation; ever since, many (but not all) prominent business leaders and organizations have taken a "go slow" approach to expanding government welfare and health programs. The minimum necessary public welfare to preserve social order seems to have been the rule in many Chamber of Commerce circles.

Even the liberal approach to federal government intervention developed since the 1930s has not been much different in its basic motivation from the conservative approach. The liberal concern with the "welfare state," as it relates to the poor, also seems to be motivated by an interest in remaking the poor or in protecting inequality. Liberal reformers have been prisoners of the capitalistic system, a social and economic framework of inequality which insures that all reform will be modest and will only slightly reduce the unequal distribution of power and privilege. The primary emphasis is on expanding the economy and using spillover growth for the poor. Moreover, most "welfare state" programs for the poor have had their wings clipped by statutes written in the spirit of individualism and the work ethic.[87]

1. W. W. Rostow, *The Stages of Economic Growth* (Cambridge: Cambridge University Press, 1962).

2. Gunnar Myrdal, *Beyond the Welfare State* (New Haven: Yale University Press, 1960), p. 62.

3. Paul A. Samuelson, *Economics* (New York: McGraw-Hill, 1973), pp. 803–5.

4. Harold L. Wilensky and Charles N. Lebeaux, *Industrial Society and Social Welfare* (New York: Free Press, 1965), pp. xvi–xvii.

5. Richard E. Edgar, *Urban Power and Social Welfare* (Beverly Hills, Calif.: Sage Publications, 1970), p. 10.

6. Richard C. Edwards, "Who Fares Well in the Welfare State?" in *The Capitalist System*, ed. Richard C. Edwards et al. (Englewood Cliffs, N.J.: Prentice-Hall, Inc., 1972), p. 244.

7. U.S. Bureau of the Census, *Statistical Abstract of the United States: 1971* (Washington, D.C.: U.S. Government Printing Office, 1971), p. 317. See also Wilensky and Lebeaux, *Industrial Society and Social Welfare*, p. 159.

8. Robert M. O'Neil, *The Price of Dependency* (New York: E. P. Dutton, 1970), p. 292.

9. A Dale Tussing, "The Dual Welfare System," *Society*, 11 (January/February 1974), 53.

10. Milwaukee County Welfare Rights Organization, *Welfare Mothers Speak Out* (New York: W. W. Norton, 1972), p. 21 and footnote 10.

11. *Ibid.*, pp. 17–21; also Philip M. Stern, *The Rape of the Taxpayer* (New York: Random House, 1973), pp. 60–306.

12. Ralph Miliband, *The State in Capitalist Society* (London: Weidenfield and Nicholson, 1969), p. 78.

13. Tussing, "The Dual Welfare System," 52–53. See also Wilensky and Lebeaux, *Industrial Society and Social Welfare*, p. xiii.

14. Tussing, "The Dual Welfare System," 51–57.

15. Neil Gilbert and Harry Specht, *Dimensions of Social Welfare Policy* (Englewood Cliffs, N.J.: Prentice-Hall, Inc., 1974), p. 3.

16. Mayer N. Zald, ed., *Social Welfare Institutions* (New York: Wiley, 1965), p. 3.

17. Wilensky and Lebeaux, *Industrial Society and Social Welfare*, pp. 138–40.

18. F. J. Peirce, "A Functional Perspective of Social Welfare," in *Perspectives on Social Welfare*, ed. Paul E. Weinberger (New York: Macmillan, 1974), p. 40.

19. Miliband, *The State in Capitalist Society*, pp. 109–10.

20. Frances F. Piven and Richard A. Cloward, *Regulating the Poor* (New York: Pantheon Books, 1971), p. xiii.

21. *Ibid.*, pp. xii ff.

22. Peirce, "A Functional Prospective of Social Welfare," pp. 44–45.

23. In revising and expanding an earlier version of Figure 1, I was influenced in part by the work of Goodwin, who diagrammed the components of welfare as a basis for suggesting experimental research. See Leonard Goodwin, "Bridging the Gap Between Research and Public Policy: Welfare, a Case in Point," *The Journal of Applied Behavioral Science*, 9 (1973), 85–114.

24. Piven and Cloward, *Regulating the Poor*, pp. 114–16.

25. U.S. Department of Health, Education and Welfare, *Social Welfare Expenditures under Public Programs in the United States, 1929–1966* (Washington, D.C.: U.S. Government Printing Office, 1968), pp. 74–77.

26. *Ibid.*, pp. 91–92.

27. U.S. Congress, Joint Economic Committee, *Studies in Public Welfare*, Paper No. 7, *Issues in the Coordination of Welfare Programs*, "Current Public Assistance Benefits and an Assessment of State Supplementation under Proposed Federal Alternatives," by Irene Lurie (Washington, D.C.: U.S. Government Printing Office, 1973), p. 235.

28. "States have the option to include in the new MA programs persons who would qualify under one of the cash assistance programs except for the fact they can provide for their own maintenance needs although not their medical care needs." This is the program for the "medically indigent." Department of Health, Education and Welfare, *Social Welfare Expenditures*, p. 77.

29. Joint Economic Committee, *Issues in the Coordination of Welfare Programs*, "Public Medical Programs and Cash Assistance: The Problems of Program Integration," by Theodore R. Marmor, p. 86.

30. Gilbert Y. Steiner, *Social Insecurity* (Chicago: Rand McNally, 1966), pp. 40–45.

31. Quoted in U.S. Congress, Joint Economic Committee, *Studies in Public Welfare*, Paper No. 5 (Part 2), *Issues in Welfare Administration*, "Public Assistance and Social Services," by Joseph Hofferman (Washington, D.C.: U.S. Government Printing Office, 1973), p. 114.

32. Steiner, *Social Insecurity*, p. 34; see also pp. 46–47.

33. Clair Wilcox, *Toward Social Welfare* (Homewood, Ill.: Irwin, 1969), p. 245.

34. Joel F. Handler, *Reforming the Poor* (New York: Basic Books, 1972), pp. 40–42.

35. U.S. Congress, Joint Economic Committee, Studies in Public Welfare, Paper No. 3, *The Effectiveness of Manpower Training Programs*, by Jon H. Goldstein (Washington, D.C.: U.S. Government Printing Office, 1972), p. 52.

36. Bennett Harrison, *Education, Training, and the Urban Ghetto* (Baltimore: Johns University Press, 1972), p. 143.

37. Joint Economic Committee, *Issues in Welfare Administration*, "Public Assistance and Social Services," pp. 115–16.

38. Joint Economic Committee, *Issues in Welfare Administration*, "Welfare Law," by Peter E. Sitkin, pp. 60–62.

39. Cited in *Ibid.*

40. See Steiner, *Social Insecurity*, pp. 18–59.

41. *Ibid.*, p. 85.

42. See Joint Economic Committee, *Issues in Welfare Administration*, "Federal-State Interests in Welfare Administration," by Joel F. Handler, pp. 1–10.

43. Steiner, *Social Insecurity*, pp. 87–89.

44. *Ibid.*, pp. 95–97.

45. U.S. Department of Health, Education and Welfare, *Social Welfare Expenditures*, pp. 74–77.

46. Wilcox, *Toward Social Welfare*, p. 230.

47. President's Commission on Income Maintenance Programs, *Poverty Amid Plenty* (Washington, D.C.: U.S. Government Printing Office, 1969), p. 117.

48. Steiner, *Social Insecurity*, p. 205.

49. Piven and Cloward, *Regulating the Poor*, p. 116.

50. Texas State Department of Public Welfare, *1971 Annual Report* (Austin, Texas: 1971), pp. 114–17. The figures come from federal data.

51. Steiner, *Social Insecurity*, p. 108.

52. Winifred Bell, *Aid to Dependent Children* (New York: Columbia University Press, 1965), p. 34.

53. *Ibid.*, p. 57.

54. *Ibid.*, pp. 138–39.

55. *Ibid.*, pp. 139–48; also Steiner, *Social Insecurity*, pp. 99–101.

56. Steiner, *Social Insecurity*, pp. 114–15.

57. *Ibid.*, pp. 118–20.

58. Wilcox, *Toward Social Welfare*, p. 236.

59. See Steiner, *Social Insecurity*, p. 124, for a discussion of less extreme birth control actions.

60. *Ibid.*, p. 140.

61. Edgar May, *The Wasted Americans* (New York: Signet Books, 1964), p. 31.

62. *Ibid.*, pp. 34–42.

63. *Ibid.*, pp. 42–45.

64. Handler, *Reforming the Poor*, p. 71.

65. See Joint Economic Committee, *Issues in Welfare Administration*, "Welfare Law," pp. 36–54.

66. Handler, *Reforming the Poor*, p. 71.

67. See evidence for this in Joint Economic Committee, *Issues in Welfare Administration*, "Welfare Law," p. 52.

68. *Ibid.*, p. 40.

69. *Ibid.*, pp. 45–46.

70. *Ibid.*, p. 38.

71. Piven and Cloward, *Regulating the Poor*, p. 308.

72. Joint Economic Committee, *Issues in Welfare Administration*, "Legislative, Administrative, and Judicial Changes in the AFDC Program, 1967–1971," by Irene Lurie, pp. 104–7.

73. Joint Economic Committee, *Studies in Public Welfare*, Paper No. 10, *The New Supplemental Security Income Program—Impact on Current Benefits and Unresolved Issues*, by James R. Storey and Irene Cox (Washington, D.C.: U.S. Government Printing Office, 1973), pp. 1–7.

74. Steiner, *Social Insecurity*, pp. 155–59.

75. Piven and Cloward, *Regulating the Poor*, pp. 206–8, 321–27.

76. *Ibid.,* pp. 324–27.

77. Larry R. Jackson and William A. Johnson, *Protest by the Poor* (New York: Rand Corporation 1973), p. ix.

78. See Milwaukee County Welfare Rights Organization, *Welfare Mothers Speak Out*; and Helen Levens, "Organizational Affiliation and Powerlessness: A Case Study of the Welfare Poor," *Social Problems*, 16 (Summer 1968), 18–32.

79. Gilbert Y. Steiner, *The State of Welfare* (Washington, D.C.: The Brookings Institution, 1971), p. 313.

80. This discussion is based on mimeographed newsletters sent out by NWRO.

81. This discussion of the secondary labor markets draws heavily on Harrison, *Education, Training, and the Urban Ghetto*, pp. 123–43.

82. David M. Gordon, *Theories of Poverty and Underemployment* (Lexington, Mass.: D. C. Heath, 1972), pp. 68 ff.

83. *Ibid.*, pp. 68–74.

84. Edwards, "Who Fares Well in the Welfare State?" *The Capitalist System*, p. 250.

85. Harrison, *Education, Training, and the Urban Ghetto*, p. 138.

86. See Goodwin, "Bridging the Gap between Social Research and Public Policy," pp. 89–90.

87. See Edgar, *Urban Power and Social Welfare*, p. 185.

4

The Ideology of Individualism: Views of the Poor

Why has the United States been a reluctant welfare state? Why has welfare for the poor traditionally been so restricted and controversial? Why has the welfare system often been used to reform the morals and values of the very poor? Certainly these are important questions; partial answers have been suggested in previous chapters. One suggested source of this restrictiveness and controversy is the economic interest of the governing elite expressed in concrete action to limit aid in order to maintain the status quo. Yet another important and closely related source can be found in America's basic value system, variously termed the work ethic, the Protestant Ethic, the achievement ideology, or the ideology of individualism. Underlying fundamental American institutions, this ideology has been viewed as including at least the following pivotal beliefs:[1]

1. That each individual should work hard and strive to succeed in competition with others;
2. That those who work hard should be rewarded with success (seen as wealth, property, prestige, and power);

This chapter draws heavily on the author's unpublished research report submitted to NIMH, entitled "American Attitudes toward Poverty and Anti-Poverty Programs" (Austin: University of Texas, 1971). Some of the findings published here have been discussed in two earlier articles: "America's Welfare Stereotypes," *Social Science Quarterly*, 52 (March 1972), 921–33; and "Poverty: We Still Believe that God Helps Those Who Help Themselves," *Psychology Today*, 6 (November 1972), 101–10, 129. The survey was supported by NIMH research grant MH15917.

3. That because of widespread and equal opportunity those who work hard will in fact be rewarded with success;

4. That economic failure is an individual's own fault and reveals lack of effort and other character defects.

Closely related to these individualistic beliefs are others relating to private property and free enterprise, which we can do no more than mention here. These critical values, which still seem strong and widely influential, are the focus of this chapter; their importance in earlier centuries of capitalist development was noted in Chapter 2.[2]

Particularly relevant for our purposes here is the belief that those who are economically unsuccessful, the poor, must bear that responsibility themselves. With the emphasis on the ideology of individualism, a development which paralleled the further growth of capitalism, came not only the positive view of the successful as virtuous but also the negative or critical view of poverty as punishment for those who were not virtuous. Bremner has summed up the nineteenth-century view of poverty as follows:

Indigence was simply the punishment meted out to the improvident by their own lack of industry and efficiency. . . . Poverty is unnecessary (for Americans), but the varying ability and virtue of men make its presence inevitable; this is a desirable state of affairs, since without the fear of want the masses would not work and there would be no incentive for the able to demonstrate their superiority; where it exists, poverty is usually a temporary problem and, both in its cause and cure, it is always an individual matter.[3]

This accentuated gospel of self-help was particularly appropriate for the exploration of the frontier and the resurgent economic development of the nineteenth century; dominant business groups and intellectual supporters such as the social Darwinists widely heralded this essentially conservative creed. Individualism became a national passion. A distinctive American folk hero developed in this period: the self-made, rags-to-riches Horatio Alger type. Yet deeply worked into the texture of the American belief system there was also a folk villain: the self-made lazy and immoral poor person. The welfare poor seem to be the most commonly cited examples of this folk villain.

A RECENT NATIONWIDE SURVEY

But what about the individualistic ethic in the contemporary United States? Until quite recently, attention to views of the poor in general and the welfare poor in particular in the mid-twentieth century had generally been limited to impressionistic comments by acute observers of the American scene, such as the following:

The belief that virtue will be rewarded and that success attends upon effort dies hard; and in our culture failure is still more likely to be charged to defect of character than to blind fate, capricious accident, or impersonalized social and economic forces.[4]

Our interest in these fundamental American beliefs prompted a nationwide opinion survey of public views in the spring of 1969.[5] A basic purpose of this survey was to investigate beliefs about the poor and poverty, with a special focus on the ideology of individualism. It also probed attitudes toward traditional welfare programs and toward three alternative income support proposals—a guaranteed-job plan, a guaranteed-income plan, and an equal-income plan. The respondents were 1,017 adults from all regions of the United States, randomly selected to represent a cross-section of the American people. The survey results give a profile of beliefs about poverty, welfare, and new alternatives to welfare—a profile showing the persistence of the individualistic ethic.

CHARACTERISTICS AND INCOME LEVELS

When the average American thinks about a poor person, what characteristics come to mind? To find out, we asked the following open-ended question: "If you were asked to describe a typical poor person in this area, how would you do it?" Most respondents gave more than one response to this question. By far the most frequent were citations of material and visible characteristics: inadequate clothing (mentioned by 28 percent of the respondents), inadequate housing (27 percent), lack of money (25 percent), and inadequate food (23 percent). Clearly, these Americans did view success as a "tangible package";[6] descriptions of the unsuccessful gave particular emphasis to material characteristics such as property, consumer goods, and income. Relatively smaller proportions of the sample cited character traits of the poor in response to this question or mentioned structural factors such as unemployment or racial discrimination in situations surrounding the poor. At this point in the interview most were not moved to comment on the causes of deprivation, but were content to underline visible and tangible characteristics.

The materialistic character of the dominant view of the poor can also be seen in responses to a question relating to the poverty-line figure widely used by federal government agencies since the mid-1960s. Each person was asked if he or she considered an average family of four in that area with a yearly income of $3,500 as poor or not poor. The overwhelming majority said that in their judgment such a family was indeed poor. This $3,500 figure was intentionally chosen to be slightly under the much-utilized government poverty line for that year. In fact, more than half the respondents agreed that such a family was poor even if its yearly income was $4,500. Thus the majority of Americans in this nationwide survey, most of whom were neither very poor nor very rich, saw the government poverty line as much too low. Here is major evidence that federal government discussions of poverty often underestimate the poverty line in the United States as it would be defined by average Americans.

What proportion of Americans are poor? Estimates by the majority of the sample were roughly similar to the widely circulated federal government figures of 10 to 15 percent, based on the federal poverty line at that time. Almost two-thirds put the figure in the 5 to 20 percent range. Most rejected estimates of the proportion in poverty that were smaller or larger than this. Only 2 percent said that poverty was virtually nonexistent in the United States, and less than one-fifth said that half the population could be considered as poor. In this case, estimates did not differ markedly from published government figures, a correspondence which may be explained by numerous mass media discussions of such figures. However, government figures understate the extent of poverty as measured by a poverty line higher than the federal government line, such as the $4,500 figure most of these respondents considered to be a poverty income.

CAUSES OF POVERTY

A major purpose of the nationwide survey was to examine beliefs about the causes of poverty in the United States. Several commentators on the American scene have argued on the basis of impressionistic evidence that an individualistic perspective is still strongly entrenched in common views on the poor. As we noted previously, Williams has suggested that failure is "still more likely to be charged to the defect of character than to blind fate, capricious accident, or impersonalized social and economic forces."

To find out whether or not the individualistic ideology was still prevalent, we asked the respondents to evaluate the importance of a list of "reasons some people give to explain why there are poor people in this country." Table 1 lists the reasons, ranked in the order of importance given to them by the respondents. The reasons are paraphrases of explanations given in pretest interviews conducted in the Los Angeles area or of interpretations common in public discussions of poverty. They can be grouped into three broad categories: (1) *individualistic explanations,* which place the responsibility for poverty primarily on the poor themselves; (2) *structural explanations,* which blame external social and economic forces; and (3) *fatalistic explanations,* which cite such factors as bad luck, illness, and the like. As predicted, individualistic explanations received the greatest emphasis. About half the sample evaluated lack of thrift, laziness, and loose morals—individualistic factors—as *very* important reasons for poverty. Significantly less emphasis, on the average, was given to structural factors, ranging from the 42 percent who saw low wages as a very important cause of poverty to the 27 percent who stressed the failure of private industry and the 18 percent who emphasized exploitation by the rich. Fatalistic explanations varied greatly in the degree of importance which the sample attached to them. Half thought that lack of talent was a critical source of poverty, while only 8 percent gave emphasis to the role of bad luck. Explanations that commonly underline lack of ability and talent as causes of poverty are similar in some ways to individualistic explanations, because they take the heat off social and economic conditions and concentrate on personal qualities. Yet, unlike individualistic explanations, these fatalistic explanations of poverty take into consideration factors more or less beyond the control of individuals—factors that cannot be remedied by moral conversion. However, they differ from structural interpretations in that the blame for poverty is not charged to flaws in the society.

Utilizing these eleven items, three *exploratory indexes* were created for further analysis. The three items that locate responsibility for poverty in the character of poor individuals (items 1, 2, and 4 in Table 1) made up the individualistic-factors index; the five items relating to aspects of the economic or social system generally beyond the control of the poor themselves (items 6 through 10) constituted the structural-factors index; the three items (3, 5, and 11) citing nonstructural factors more or less beyond the control of individuals were placed together in a fatalistic-factors index.[7] Scores on each item were summed to get a total score for each respondent. Equivalent cutting points were used to determine low, medium, and high placement on each of the three indexes for each person in the sample, based on total index scores. Although just over half of the respondents scored high on the individualistic-factors index, only a minority scored high on the other two. The index with the highest proportion falling in the very low emphasis category (18 percent) was the structural-factors index. On the average, individualistic factors were considered considerably more important than were structural or fatalistic factors in explaining contemporary poverty. This confirms the impression gained from looking at the pattern for the eleven individual items in Table 1.

In the historical study of approaches to poverty cited previously, Bremner concludes that by the turn of the century an extremely individualistic interpretation of poverty and its causes was firmly entrenched in the dominant belief system. Above all, in the nineteenth-century view, poverty, "both in its cause and its cure,"

TABLE 1
REASONS FOR POVERTY

Reasons for Poverty	Percentage Replying				
	Very Important	Somewhat Important	Not Important	Uncertain	Total
1. Lack of thrift and proper money management by poor people	58%	30%	11%	2%	101%*
2. Lack of effort by the poor themselves	55	33	9	3	100%
3. Lack of ability and talent among poor people	52	33	12	3	100%
4. Loose morals and drunkenness	48	31	17	4	100%
5. Sickness and physical handicaps	46	39	14	2	101%
6. Low wages in some businesses and industries	42	35	20	3	100%
7. Failure of society to provide good schools for many Americans	36	25	34	5	100%
8. Prejudice and discrimination against Negroes	33	37	26	5	101%
9. Failure of private industry to provide enough jobs	27	36	31	6	100%
10. Being taken advantage of by rich people	18	30	45	7	100%
11. Just bad luck	8	27	60	5	100%

* Some totals do not add to exactly 100 percent because of statistical rounding procedures.

was seen as "an individual matter." Judging from the survey data, such a creed is still common. Although half of the entire sample placed great emphasis on individualistic factors, such as lack of effort and lack of personal thrift, only a minority viewed societal factors to be of equal importance. Although the structural interpretation seems to have emerged in the last several decades as an increasingly important view of poverty, as given some credence by many in this sample, it is clear that the individualistic view is still firmly entrenched among average Americans.

SOURCES OF POVERTY
INTERPRETATIONS

What are the social and economic sources of these interpretations? Are some groups in this society more likely to rely on individualistic explanations than others? These are important questions. Analysis of socioeconomic and demographic subgroups in the sample revealed that emphatic individualism was not scattered at random. Nor was thoroughgoing structuralism. Subgroups varied greatly in the extent to which they underscored different views. Members of certain groups were significantly more likely than others to be highly individualistic in their views of the poor. The basic patterns can be seen in Table 2. Groups with the largest concentrations of persons giving high priority to individualistic explanations were:

1. White Protestants and Catholics
2. Residents of the South and North Central regions
3. The over-50 age group
4. The middle-income group
5. Groups with middle levels of education

In contrast, the groups with the largest proportions ranking high on structuralism were:

1. Black Protestants and Jews
2. The under-30 age group
3. The low-income group
4. The less well-educated

Although there are some supporters of emphatic individualism and structuralism in all segments of American society, these data point to the conclusion that major strongholds of individualism are to be found among whites, Southerners, older Americans, and those at the middle socioeconomic levels, while the strongholds of emphatic structuralism are among nonwhite and Jewish Americans, the young, and those at low socioeconomic levels. We can now examine

TABLE 2
SOURCES OF SUPPORT FOR POVERTY EXPLANATIONS

	Percent *High* on Individualistic-Factors Index	Percent *High* on Fatalistic-Factors Index	Percent *High* on Structural-Factors Index
Socioreligious Group			
white Protestant (*N* = 538)*	59%	17%	15%
white Catholic (*N* = 213)	53	21	19
black Protestant (*N* = 108)	47	26	57
Jewish (*N* = 26)	35	12	39
Racial Group			
white (*N* = 830)	56	18	17
black (*N* = 120)	45	25	54
other (*N* = 45)	24	15	28
Region			
Northeast (*N* = 239)	42	16	21
North Central (*N* = 287)	58	18	18
South (*N* = 296)	61	21	24
West (*N* = 181)	46	18	26
Age			
under 30 (*N* = 229)	42	9	25
30–49 (*N* = 373)	50	18	21
over 50 (*N* = 401)	62	24	21
Family Income			
under $4000 (*N* = 271)	51	25	28
$4000–5999 (*N* = 155)	57	18	20
$6000–9999 (*N* = 279)	55	18	23
$10,000 or more (*N* = 284)	50	12	16
Education			
6th grade or less (*N* = 108)	52	31	24
7–11th grade (*N* = 341)	60	21	25
12th grade, technical school (*N* = 319)	54	16	21
some college or more (*N* = 224)	42	12	18

* *N*s presented are for the individualistic-factors index; they vary a little for the other two indexes. Some social categories (such as the nonreligious and no response) have been excluded for this table.

three of these variables—socioreligious group, income, and education—a bit further.

Religion is an important source of individualistic views, as suggested by a number of scholars since the turn of the century. In *The Protestant Ethic and the Spirit of Capitalism* Max Weber argued that there was an intimate relationship between basic Protestant beliefs about individual effort and work (work seen as a duty and a calling) and the rise of Western capitalism.[8] Inspired by Weber, one contemporary researcher in a study in Detroit, Michigan found that white Protestants and Jews were more likely to hold to individualistic, competition-oriented attitudes than other socioreligious groups such as white Catholics and black Protestants.[9] Examining the data in Table 2 we note here only a little support for the prediction, drawn from Weber and Lenski, that white Protestants would place greater emphasis on individualistic explanations than would white Catholics. Fifty-nine percent of the white Protestants were emphatic in their individualism, compared to 53 percent of the white Catholics. The difference between these two groups is small; on this issue the Protestant-Catholic cleavage no longer seems important. Both white groups stressed individualistic explanations more than black Protestants, but the black-white difference was modest. Jewish respondents were the least likely to place great emphasis on individualistic factors.

In addition, the Jewish respondents ranked second to the blacks, and well ahead of the white Protestants and Catholics, in emphasizing structural interpretations. Black Protestants and Jews placed less emphasis on individualistic factors and much greater emphasis on structural factors than the other groups. Interestingly, those groups placing the greatest emphasis on societal conditions as generating poverty are two of America's most discussed minority groups—groups that have suffered significant discrimination over the last century. Doubtless, the combination of discriminatory experiences in this society and the emergence of civil rights organizations with structure-oriented ideologies has led many black and Jewish citizens to view economic failure in a different light. In this regard, religion seems less important than recent minority status.

The findings on income and education also deserve additional comment. Among the background variables frequently investigated by social scientists are indicators of class such as income and education. Income was expected to be strongly associated with views of poverty, with the poor being more likely than the more advantaged to emphasize structural and fatalistic explanations and less likely to underscore individualistic interpretations. The reasoning here was that the poor person, more aware of the victimization, would place significantly greater emphasis on societal factors, whereas those more advantaged would emphasize individualistic factors. Yet the data reveal little difference between the four income groups in emphasis on individualistic factors; the pattern is curvilinear, with 50 to 51 percent of both the lowest-income group (less than $4,000) and the highest-income group ($10,000 or more) scoring high on the individualistic factors index. The in-between groups were just a little more likely than the income extremes to score high on the individualistic-factors index. The pattern on the other two indexes is roughly as expected. The low-income group gave greater emphasis to structural factors than the affluent, while the other income groups fell into a stair-step pattern. The poor were also more likely to emphasize fatalistic factors than the affluent; again the other income groups fell in between. Thus the widespread dominance of emphatic individualism seems obvious in these data.

Moreover, those with relatively poor educations, because of their experience, were expected to place less stress on individualism and greater emphasis on structural and fatalistic factors than their more advantaged brethren. Yet the survey results do not show a consistent pattern in regard to education. Looking at the structural-factors index, we see that the pattern is roughly as predicted, with the less-educated placing a little greater emphasis on structural factors than those with a high school or college degree. A similar pattern was found in the case of the fatalistic factors; in that case the less-educated placed significantly greater emphasis on such things as illness and bad luck than the better-educated. And the proportion high in individualism decreases with increases in education, except for the most poorly educated, who rank lower than those at middle levels. While emphatic individualism has a pervasive influence cutting across class lines (measured by income or education)—and this is an important finding here—still those less advantaged in terms of income and education are somewhat more likely than more advantaged groups to emphasize structural and fatalistic factors, to underscore circumstances beyond the control of the poor.

It may be that the *very* rich, much too small a group in this sample to be analyzed separately here, would place far more emphasis on individualistic explanations, and less on system-blame explanations, than do any of these poor or middle-income groups.

Recently, researchers in Muskegon, Michigan interviewed a sample of rich Americans and found them to be significantly more individualistic in their views of poverty than those in low-income and middle-income groups, while differences between these latter two groups were modest.[10] Further research on the ideologies of the very rich and of the ruling elites, a segment of the population greatly neglected by survey researchers, is needed.

WELFARE: THE RANK-AND-FILE VIEW

About welfare? What do I think about the welfare? It ought to be cut back. The goddamn people sit around when they should be working and then they're having illegitimate kids to get more money. You know, their morals are different. They don't give a damn.[11]

Such was the assessment given by a cab driver to Edgar May, a journalist who has written pioneering articles on welfare. Public and private discussion of welfare such as this usually relates to the public assistance provided to the poor by welfare agencies. Over the last few decades numerous charges have been directed at the welfare poor—their improper work attitudes, their illegitimate children, their immorality, and their excessive incomes. Another major objective of our 1969 nationwide survey was to find out just how widespread these traditional negative criticisms of welfare are.

We asked our respondents across the country to evaluate several statements about welfare and welfare recipients; the statements were drawn in part from earlier research by Kallen and Miller.[12] These statements and the responses to them can be seen in Table 3. The response percentages which reflect or suggest the *traditional* positions critical of welfare recipients and programs are italicized. In every case but one a plurality of this cross-section of Americans took a traditional anti-welfare position; and in four cases a majority took the traditional position. Also, in every case but one, the percentage of the sample that was willing to give a "don't know" or "not sure" response was relatively small. In their earlier study Kallen and Miller found similarly strong acceptance of conventional welfare stereotypes among two samples in Maryland.

TABLE 3
ATTITUDES TOWARD WELFARE

Attitudes	Percentage Replying			
	Agree	Disagree	Uncertain	Total
1. There are too many people receiving welfare money who should be working.	84%	11%	5%	100%
2. Many people getting welfare are *not* honest about their need.	71	17	12	100%
3. Many women getting welfare money are having illegitimate babies to increase the money they get.	61	23	16	100%
4. Generally speaking, we are spending too *little* money on welfare programs in this country.	34	54	13	101%
5. Most people on welfare who can work try to find jobs so they can support themselves.	43	49	8	100%
6. One of the main troubles with welfare is that it doesn't give people enough to get along on.	45	43	12	100%
7. A lot of people are moving to this state from other states just to get welfare money here.	41	31	28	100%

STEREOTYPES OR ACCURATE GENERALIZATIONS?

To what extent are the traditional anti-welfare views true? Are they negative stereotypes—that is, exaggerated beliefs negatively associated with a social category? What is the fit between the traditional anti-welfare arguments suggested by the survey items and the reality of welfare programs as reflected in administrative data and in various research studies? We will now examine some evidence relevant both to the explicit arguments about welfare imbedded in the survey questions and to other closely related assertations about welfare programs and recipients. (The headings which follow are stated in the anti-welfare directions.)

There are too many people receiving welfare money who should be working. Eighty-four percent of the nationwide sample agreed with this generalization. Such a statement about welfare recipients usually goes along with other negative assertions to the effect that the majority of those on welfare rolls could easily be removed and put to work at a living wage in the present economy. In Chapter 3 we saw the importance of these views in local and congressional actions.

Yet this general attitude reflects a basic misunderstanding about who receives welfare aid. Available data indicate that relatively few welfare recipients can be considered readily employable at a living wage in the current economy. To illustrate, according to one federal government study the distribution of welfare recipients receiving money payments in the year of the survey (November 1969) was roughly as follows: (1) AFDC children (49 percent); (2) elderly persons (19 percent); (3) parents in families with AFDC children (17 percent); (4) permanent or totally disabled people (6 percent); (5) blind people (1 percent); (7) those on general assistance (8 percent).[13] Most welfare recipients were either blind, disabled, elderly, or children.

Parents in the AFDC families have been the most likely target for work ethic criticisms of welfare. Who are these parents, and what is their employment status? Only a small minority of AFDC families have unemployed, able-bodied fathers. Half the states do not make AFDC grants to families with fathers present; in the remaining states, typically, a small minority (often about 10 percent) of AFDC families have fathers present. Among the fathers who receive welfare aid the majority have age or health problems or no marketable skills; and some are already working at wages so low that their families still qualify for some low public assistance payments.[14] Reports since the late 1960s have noted that able-bodied men accounted for less than 1 percent of the nation's welfare recipients. "Most of them—80 percent—want work, according to a Government-sponsored study; about half the men are enrolled in work training programs." [15] Eligibility for payments requires most of them to be actively seeking work. In spite of these documented facts, most Americans continue to *overestimate* greatly the proportion of relief recipients who are able-bodied, unemployed males. One investigator recently surveyed a large sample of average Bostonians, asking for estimates of the percentage of welfare recipients who are able-bodied males.[16] Remarkably, the average estimate was *37 percent*, far in excess of the actual figure.

A recent HEW review of AFDC mothers estimated that: (1) 28 percent of the total were working at low-wage jobs, enrolled in work training programs, or actively seeking work; (2) another 22 percent had significant mental or physical incapacities or no marketable skills; and (3) 39 percent were needed at home as full-time homemakers, mainly because of small children or the lack of child-care facilities. Only a small percentage did not fall into these categories.[17] Moreover, the typical mother on welfare has little in the way of assets or resources other than welfare to draw on; and she typically has little in the way of marketable skills or education. Even if jobs were somehow made available in an accessible area, it is probable that the skill level of most welfare mothers would entitle them only to irregular jobs or those paying a meager wage.

One of the most important assumptions underlying the work ethic critique of the welfare poor is the assumption that decent-paying jobs are readily available for able-bodied recipients who seek them. Yet this seems a wrong assumption. Work histories of recipients usually reveal fruitless job searching, production cutbacks resulting in unemployment, and marginal part-time jobs. In an economy where skilled white male workers often face high levels of unemployment, unskilled women workers have far greater difficulty locating jobs both in rural and urban areas. Writing in the 1970s, one author has suggested that "with over 5 million unemployed in the labor market, it seems preposterous to assume that job vacancies exist in abundance for those on welfare. Even if some vacancies did appear, the competition from more advantaged workers would be intense under these labor market conditions." [18] As we have noted previously, in spite of new government training programs, including those for welfare recipients, there has been much reluctance on the part of employers in hiring the newly trained welfare poor at levels above the secondary labor market.

Most people on welfare who can work do not try to find jobs so they can support themselves. This criticism of work *attitudes* is also tied to the issue of employability. The 1969 survey dropped the "not" out of the statement and asked respondents if they agreed with the sentence, "Most people on welfare who can work try to find jobs so they can support themselves." More disagreed than agreed with this positive view.

To what extent have welfare recipients tried to work? What are the barriers to finding employment? Do recipients reject the work ethic? Of those welfare recipients who are able to work, some are presently working and still eligible, because of very low wages, to receive public assistance. Studies have shown a minority are presently working full- or part-time or are in work training programs.[19] Moreover, one nationwide survey of over 5,000 AFDC recipients found that two-thirds had been employed for some portion of the three-year period preceding the interview.[20] For most, work patterns were seasonal or irregular; only 9 percent of these low-income mothers had been employed for the entire three-year period. For many, work and welfare were alternative means of economic existence; for some, welfare supplemented low wages. Realistic reasons were usually given for periods of unemployment and dependence on welfare: poor health, the lack of child care, the inability to find work. The same study also found a high correlation between level of education, one measure of job-related skills, and the number of months worked prior to the interview. Again, public assistance did not seem to be a refuge for those who do not work, but a place of last resort for those who cannot work or who cannot find work.

Nor do the attitudes of typical welfare recipients seem anti-work or oriented toward laziness and delight with welfare living. One well-conceived study of welfare mothers in New York found that *seven in ten* said they would rather work for pay than stay at home on welfare.[21] The majority who preferred to stay at home cited child care, housework, and health as reasons. Even a majority of mothers with preschool children (about two-thirds of all mothers on welfare in New York City) said that they would prefer to work if there were a good place to leave children all day. The same study found that two-thirds of the women on welfare expected to work for pay in the future.

Reviewing a number of studies of work motivation among the poor, Schiller found little difference between the employed and nonemployed poor. "What distinguishes the employed from the nonemployed poor at any point in time is not the work ethic, but a combination of job opportunities and demographic problems." [22] He further notes that a few studies have even indicated that poor people have a somewhat *stronger* orientation to work than those in other income groups. One of the best of these work orientation studies is an extensive one by Leonard Goodwin, simply entitled *Do the Poor Want to Work?* Goodwin found that the poor—young and old, black and white—were very work-oriented and had as high aspirations as the nonpoor. "This study reveals no differences between poor and nonpoor when it comes to life goals and wanting to work." [23] Even long-term welfare mothers and their teenage sons were strongly work-oriented and did not need instruction in the work ethic. Goodwin suggests that the way to encourage entry into the labor force is to provide them "a chance to experience success in jobs that will support them." [24] Moreover, another important study in California found that three-quarters of the welfare mothers interviewed had significant motivation to become self-supporting, as evaluated by a panel of medical and occupational experts. [25] As a group they were work-oriented, but barriers of skills and child-care arrangements again intervened.

In addition, a few studies have found a negative attitude toward being on welfare among many recipients; a majority of the welfare mothers interviewed in a New York study felt that "getting money from welfare makes a person feel ashamed." [26] This feeling may account for the fact that a large proportion of those who have not found decent-paying jobs have not, over the last few decades, gone on welfare even though they qualify.

Many people getting welfare money are not honest about their need. In our nationwide survey nearly three-quarters of those interviewed accepted this contention; only a small minority disagreed. Moreover, in another recent study one researcher asked a large Boston sample, "What percent of welfare recipients lie about their financial situation?" [27] The average estimate in this liberal city was a rather high *41 percent.* Strong public adherence to the ancient view that a very large proportion of recipients (the majority, for many Americans) are criminally inclined chiselers or dishonest loafers persists. Intentional fraud is considered to be very widespread. Such arguments are often used to explain why the welfare rolls are large, or why they have grown. But they seem questionable in light of available data.

One federal study of random samples of welfare recipients in all states revealed that most states had technically ineligible proportions of less than 6 percent.[28] The national figure was 5 percent. Further examination revealed that the proportion ineligible because of agency error was higher than the proportion ineligible because of client error, most of which probably could not be construed as intentional fraud. Not surprisingly, ineligibility figures have tended to be the highest where caseloads were high and payments were low relative to costs.[29] A 1971 HEW study produced similar findings, with approximately 5 percent found to be ineligible on a nationwide basis, the majority because of agency error.[30] Errors by recipients were found to include incorrect or incomplete information, as well as the failure to report changes in economic circumstances. Given the complexity of welfare rules and regulations, neither the agency nor the client errors seem especially surprising. Most low-income people have a great deal of difficulty in dealing with middle-class bureaucracies, including local welfare agencies. Even the intensive scrutiny of welfare rolls by critical HEW administrators of client error has concluded that "in most cases, there was no evidence of deliberate misrepresentation." [31]

Prosecutions for fraud, perhaps the best available data on client dishonesty, amount to less than 1 percent of all cases. State surveys have usually corroborated this picture of relatively little welfare fraud.[32] Worth noting too is the view of the honesty of welfare recipients taken by those who work closely with them. One nationwide survey of welfare caseworkers—not always the most sympathetic observers—found a substantial majority believed that few welfare recipients were dishonest.[33] While no one would suggest that fraud is absent or that welfare recipients are above reproach, the data currently available on client dishonesty and fraud suggests that it is not nearly as great as the public perceives it to be; and it appears to be a significantly lower percentage than common estimates of the proportion of Americans who cheat on income taxes.

Many women getting welfare money are having illegitimate babies to increase the money they get. In the national survey six out of ten respondents agreed with this point of view. This argument suggests that large numbers of welfare mothers are cheating by having illegitimate babies just to increase their assistance payments. It is often linked to the publicly expressed view that most welfare children are illegitimate. Yet AFDC data indicate that such arguments are questionable. Most children (an estimated 80 percent for New York) born out of wedlock do not receive public assistance aid.[34] Nor are most children on welfare illegitimate; a 1969 study found that seven in ten among the AFDC children were legitimate under state laws, some of which use a conservative definition (e.g., regarding children of common-law marriages as illegitimate).[35] And more recent figures support the findings of this 1969 study.[36] It is also important to note that family counseling, private physicians, and adoption services have not been as widely available for poor families as for middle- and upper-income families. Such a situation decreases the likelihood of concealing illegitimacy among the poor, as it has been concealed among the more affluent.

Remarkably little research has been conducted on the economic view of illegitimacy, but what there is suggests that the view is very questionable. According to a few studies most illegitimate children were born before, not after, welfare families applied for public assistance. One Utah study found that of the 13 percent of illegitimate children on welfare nine in ten among them were born before the families had applied for assistance. This is in line with national figures on welfare children indicating that the overwhelming majority of welfare children were conceived or born *before* the family applied for assistance.[37] In addition, economically this misconception seems farfetched, because the typical payment for an additional child in the early 1970s was about $35 a month, not even enough to cover rock-bottom expenses for a child.[38] A Utah welfare booklet points out that this view makes little economic sense, because a recipient mother with two children in Utah received $5 a day for all expenses (in 1967); and a third child would increase her welfare grant by only seventy cents a day.[39] Additional children would bring even smaller increases. Indeed, a number of states have had a maximum limit on family size (often four to five persons), so for many families additional children would mean *no* increased benefits. It is also interesting to note that the previously cited nationwide survey of welfare workers revealed that most disagreed with labeling welfare women as "oversexed" or "immoral," a view that seems to lie behind the charge of welfare illegitimacy for profit.[40] Few caseworkers felt that most welfare recipients could accurately be described in these terms.

Closely related to the illegitimacy issue is the question of welfare fertility. In the average American's mind the typical welfare family is *very* large. A recent survey asked a sample of Bostonians, "How many children under 18 are there in the average AFDC family?" The average estimate by respondents in this sample from a liberal state was *4.8 children.* This greatly overstates the real situation, because HEW statistics show a national average of 2.6 children per family.[41] The same survey found that 44 percent of the Boston respondents also believed the AFDC birthrate has been increasing in recent years, although it has in fact *decreased.* The Boston sample's image of large and growing families on welfare is probably prevalent throughout the United States.

A lot of people are moving to this state from other states just to get welfare money here. A plurality of the sample, 41 percent, accepted this generalization about welfare recipients, although a significant proportion expressed uncertainty in this case. This view was expressed by many respondents in *all* regions of the United States. There is a certain contradiction in the answers of respondents in various regions to this question, which can only be indirectly assessed. This argument is often linked to the idea that very recent migrants, particularly recent black migrants from the Deep South, dominate the welfare rolls. Yet until the late 1960s there were strict residency requirements for most state public assistance programs. A person moving from one state to another had to wait a lengthy period (usually one to five years) in order to qualify for any substantial public aid. However, in 1968 a Supreme Court decision had the effect of knocking down formal residency requirements for public assistance, although some states were slow to respond. Apparently, the court ruling has not greatly affected the residency characteristics of average recipients, including those in the AFDC program. An Illinois study, conducted after the Supreme Court decision, found that 96 percent of AFDC cases had resided in Illinois for at least a year before receiving aid; three-quarters had lived in the state for more than five years.[42] Earlier studies reported a similar pattern. A 1966 New York City survey revealed that three-quarters of those on welfare had been born in New York City or had lived there for at least five years.[43] Length of state residence for those on welfare programs other than AFDC tends to be even higher.[44]

At this point, research data on migration and welfare are in some ways inconclusive because no one has done a thorough longitudinal study of immigrants and their welfare views before and after their immigration from lower to higher benefit areas. However, one thing is clear: the major reasons for immigration to urban areas for the overwhelming majority of all poor and nonpoor workers studied are job-related. Tilly has summarized the research literature on migration to cities as follows:

When interviewers ask American migrants why they have moved, the migrants give answers relating to jobs far more than any other answers; the largest number usually report a specific job brought them to the city, but another sizable number say they came looking for work. This is about as true for Negroes as it is for whites.[45]

Tilly further notes that poor unskilled workers, black and white, are more likely to migrate looking for work. Why do the unskilled choose certain areas? "For people moving without a guarantee of a job the presence of friends and relatives matters a great deal more than such things as the housing supply or the availability of public assistance." [46]

Other studies have also underlined the importance of employment opportunities in the causal forces lying behind cityward migration, the type many critics of welfare seem to have most in mind. One study focusing solely on rural to urban migration—based on interviews in rural and urban areas with southeastern blacks, Appalachian whites, and southwestern Spanish Americans —probed the causes. They found that a sizable majority gave job-related reasons for moving to urban areas. Other factors that were important were the excitement and amenities of the city, including the attractions of better housing and education. Moreover, perception of the greater availability of government program "assistance in the urban area did not correlate in any consistent pattern with migration behavior." [47] In the case of the southeastern blacks the correlations between migration and positive reactions to questions bearing on government program aid in the city were negative. The results for the other two groups on potential government aid were inconsistent.

As for adjustment after migration, a number of studies have questioned the view that migrants, particularly black migrants, are more likely to be dependent on welfare assistance than others. Several important research studies have shown that most migrants soon become attached to jobs in urban areas and that their welfare rate is similar to that of the poor already in the city.[48] A recent cross-sectional analysis, using 1970 census data, revealed that black migrants to six large cities were less likely to be on welfare than native black residents, while for whites there was no consistent relationship between migration status and being on welfare. Black migrants from the South—only a portion of all black migrants— were more likely to be on welfare than natives right at first, but after a few years Southern migrants were found to be less likely to depend on welfare than the native-born.[49]

Of course, demographic studies such as these do not deal directly with whether or not higher welfare benefits played a significant role in the migration of any migrants.[50] It seems probable that most migrants who come to depend on welfare programs do so because of the serious economic and employment problems, or family difficulties, encountered in the cities to which they migrate. Taken together, these data raise serious questions about the view that lots of people are migrating just to get higher welfare benefits; it seems likely that few of those who resort to welfare in a given state at a given point in time can be accurately described as freeloaders who have heard the word about higher welfare benefits. Although the final data are not in on this issue, it does seem to be a gross exaggeration to see large swarms of the poor from other states as a major cause of welfare problems in one's own state.

One of the main troubles with welfare is that it gives people too much money to live on. In our nationwide survey a question relevant to this line of argument was asked. Forty-three percent of the sample *disagreed* with the view that "one of the main troubles with welfare is that it doesn't give people enough money to get along on." Forty-five percent agreed. This was the only item on which the proportion favorable to the problems of welfare recipients slightly exceeded the proportion taking a conventional anti-welfare position.

But do welfare recipients receive a lot of money? Do they receive more than rank-and-file workers? Can a large number afford the new "welfare Cadillacs" in the popular mythology? In the late 1960s most welfare families received less than the $3,500 a year the overwhelming majority of the nationwide sample considered to be a minimal poverty line for a family of four. That this is a rock-bottom figure is suggested by the results of a 1970 Gallup Poll, which found that most Americans felt that a family of four could not get along on less than $6,240 a year, a substantially higher "poverty line." [51] This figure is about 60 percent of the median income. We have already noted in a previous chapter that in June 1971 the average AFDC cash benefit in the United States was $183 per family, ranging from $52 in Mississippi to $266 in Hawaii. The average payments for the other categories of public aid ranged from $76 per month per family for the aged to $104 per month per recipient for the blind. Of course, these cash assistance figures were even lower in 1969 when the nationwide survey of welfare attitudes was conducted. Certainly, by the 1970s in-kind benefits (food stamps, etc.) had increased the standard of living of many recipients somewhat, but not enough to raise most welfare families above the level that middle-income Americans would consider completely inadequate. It is also important to note that in-kind benefits were not widely utilized in the late 1960s. One 1967 study of 3,000 welfare mothers found that only 24 percent had reportedly received help with medical care and 11 percent had received food.[52] Only half reported aid of any kind, including counseling, other than payments. Since the late 1960s, the time of the survey, some improvements have been made in cash and in-kind benefits, although many gains appear temporary as they have been offset by the dramatic inflation of the mid-1970s. Indeed, in the last few years most states (38 in 1971) have paid families less than their own established (and low) "need" level for welfare families, a level which officially indicates the amount necessary for the basic necessities of family living.[53]

Although some welfare families in *some* urban areas of a few states may now be able to achieve or exceed poverty-line levels if they maximize their use of all available government programs and benefits,[54] suggestions that the majority of welfare recipients live as well as the average American worker still seem ludicrous in the light of the figures on average welfare benefits. The results of living on welfare are evident in one study. A recent (1967) survey of AFDC recipients found that in the preceding six months large proportions reported they had been unable to afford medical or dental care; one-third had put off paying the rent in order to buy enough food.[55] About half the women reported that there had been times in the preceding six months when their children had gone without milk for lack of money. For most recipients welfare still means living "low on the hog." Welfare is the "good life" only for those who have not lived it.[56]

Generally speaking, we are spending too much money on welfare programs in this country. The item in the survey was phrased in the pro-welfare-recipient direction, so support for the generalization in the heading above must be inferred from the 54 percent who disagreed with the statement that "too little money" is being spent on welfare programs. This item focuses on the general level of welfare programs, not on recipients themselves, and cannot be similarly examined in light of data on recipients. Yet the traditional view of high spending does seem questionable. Because a significant proportion of those who qualify for cash welfare aid (estimated to be as high as 50 to 60 percent) were not receiving aid in 1969, and if one assumes that all of the needy poor eligible for aid have a right to receive it, welfare proponents can reasonably argue that national spending is actually much too low. Moreover, as we noted previously, the average level of payment to those poor individuals and families receiving public assistance is low; increasing the average level of cash aid even to the government's poverty-line figure would necessitate greater welfare spending.

A view related to the notion of high welfare spending is that such spending comes out of local taxes. Critics sometimes credit the high cost of local property taxes to such extravagances as welfare expenditures. However, one California study found that only 6 percent of local property tax dollars went for welfare costs.[57] The lion's share of welfare costs comes out of the federal and state government budgets, with the federal government share often taking first place.

OTHER MISCONCEPTIONS

Of course these critical misconceptions and exaggerated generalizations about welfare do not exhaust the list of such views that have been passed along in the United States for several decades now. Other stereotyped views have appeared in public discussions of welfare, including the opinion that many recipients spend much of their aid on liquor, that most recipients are second- or third-generation recipients, and that minority (particularly black) Americans constitute the majority of recipients. This list could certainly be lengthened, and it would probably vary somewhat by area of the country. Yet these conceptions too appear to be false in light of available evidence.[58] Indeed, one would be hard-pressed to find a group of American citizens who have received more hostility and criticism than have welfare clients in the last few decades. Although the sensational and grossly exaggerated stereotypes of certain minority groups, such as black Americans or Jewish Americans, have virtually disappeared from public discussion, as of the late 1960s and early 1970s this was not the case for welfare recipients. A large proportion of average Americans seem to have little concern for the facts about welfare recipients or welfare programs. On certain issues negative views of welfare are so strong that even a more reasonable "I don't know" response is rejected by the overwhelming majority.

VARIATION IN ANTI-WELFARISM

Given that the data above suggest that most conventional generalizations are either exaggerated or mythical, we also wondered about variation in traditional anti-welfare views. Do they vary within the population? As a first step toward an answer, we constructed a composite index and examined important demographic subgroups in the national sample. By scoring each respondent's responses to each of the seven items and summing the scores, we created an *exploratory* anti-welfare index indicating the extent of an individual's support for *traditional* anti-welfarism. A person high on the index typically agreed with most of the traditional anti-welfare views.[59] A person low on the index typically rejected conventional anti-welfare wisdom on most of the items. In the sample as a whole, 36 percent scored high on the index, while 25 percent scored low. Forty percent fell in between, accepting some traditional anti-welfare views and rejecting others.

There was considerable variation in anti-welfare sentiment. Groups with the largest concentrations of persons who emphatically supported traditional criticisms of welfare were:

1. White Protestants and Catholics
2. Residents of the Northeast and North Central regions
3. The over-50 age group
4. The higher-income groups
5. Groups at the middle levels of education

A comparison with the social and economic sources of the individualistic interpretation of poverty reveals that the pattern here is roughly similar. Vigorous anti-welfare sentiment was not randomly distributed. Strongholds of emphatic anti-welfarism were to be found among whites, among those in the Northern regions, older Americans, and those at middle levels of income and education. Black Americans, the young, and those in the lowest income and education groups were the least likely to consistently support conventional critiques of welfare recipients and programs.

Income and education were related to anti-welfarism in slightly different ways. There is a marked income difference in traditional

TABLE 4

VARIATION IN ANTI-WELFARE SENTIMENT

	Percent Scoring High on Index
Socioreligious Group	
white Protestant (*N* = 542)	41%
white Catholic (*N* = 218)	41
Jewish (*N* = 26)	35
Black Protestant (*N* = 110)	12
Racial Group	
white (*N* = 840)	41
black (*N* = 122)	12
other nonwhite (*N* = 47)	15
Region	
Northeast (*N* = 247)	40
North Central (*N* = 290)	37
South (*N* = 297)	34
West (*N* = 183)	30
Age	
under 30 (*N* = 232)	30
30–49 (*N* = 378)	36
50 + (*N* = 407)	39
Family Income	
under $4000 (*N* = 279)	26
$4000–5999 (*N* = 155)	35
$6000–9999 (*N* = 284)	40
$10,000 + (*N* = 285)	43
Education	
6th grade or less (*N* = 112)	30
7th–11th grade (*N* = 346)	37
12th (*N* = 322)	37
some college or more (*N* = 235)	35

anti-welfare sentiment, with the highest income group expressing the greatest negativism. Just under half (43 percent) of the affluent ($10,000 plus) group scored high on the anti-welfare index, compared to one-quarter of the low-income group. The higher an individual's income level, the more likely he or she is to have a consistently unfavorable view of welfare. One might predict that anti-welfare sentiment would be inversely related to education, because the better-educated are presumably better-informed; these survey data do not confirm such a prediction. The relationship between education and anti-welfare views is curvilinear; those respondents with the least educational attainment were also the least likely to score high on this index. Those at the middle levels were the most likely of the groups to score high, while those with college educations were only a little less likely to score high than those at the middle levels. Clearly, a large number of the best-educated Americans in this survey accepted many conventional myths and misconceptions about welfare.

In other studies, welfare views have been found to be only weakly related to conventional measures of socioeconomic status. In his recent Boston study, Williamson found that socioeconomic status did not explain much of the variation in opposition to increased welfare benefits.[60] The relationship was weak, even though the sample was intentionally stratified by socioeconomic status to check that relationship. In an earlier Baltimore study, Kallen and Miller found that a number of background variables, including education and income, did not on the whole relate to differences in welfare attitudes.[61]

ANTI-WELFARISM AND
INDIVIDUALISM

How can the persistence of these conventional anti-welfare views be explained in the last third of the twentieth century? Why do so many Americans take such a negative view of welfare? As we have seen, the overwhelming majority in the survey accepted some welfare stereotypes, and a large percentage took the traditionally critical position on most items. Such a perspective was seen to be particularly characteristic of white and nonpoor Americans. Why is traditional anti-welfare sentiment so strong among these groups? One partial explanation that has been suggested is that for white Americans such sentiment is related to anti-black prejudice; some Americans are anti-welfare because they are anti-black. Some evidence for this association was provided in a study of white women in Baltimore, where white women with anti-black attitudes were more likely than others to be anti-welfare.[62] This is a provocative explanation, and probably correct in part, but surveys have documented a precipitous decline in anti-black sentiment in the last two decades while anti-welfare sentiment appears to have remained relatively strong. Moreover, in some areas of the country where anti-welfare sentiment is very strong there are few black Americans.

Psychoanalytic explanations of anti-welfare sentiment have also been suggested. One such speculative theory has been proposed by Diamond, who argues that underlying the hostility toward welfare recipients is a half-conscious, primitive, and irrational fear that the very existence of the dregs of society, the poor, threatens the continuance of society and civilization.[63] Present welfare attitudes are seen as symptoms of a social neurosis; and negative sanctions must be used to control the feared poor. Although such speculative theories are intriguing and may well be useful in developing a comprehensive explanation, they give too much emphasis to the subconscious and to irrationality.

Perhaps a more important source of anti-welfare sentiment can be found in the basic individualism that pervades the American value system. Such an argument does not require assumptions of frustration, abnormality, or irrationality. The dominant individualistic ethic emphasizes hard work, competitive effort, and individual responsibility for failure. Deeply ingrained into the fundamental belief system is the belief in a folk villain, the self-made poor person who is lazy, immoral, and irresponsible. Views about this folk-villain myth are perhaps best exemplified in the prevailing attitudes about welfare recipients. Their problems are seen as resulting from immorality or character flaws: their unwillingness to work, their laziness, their sexual deviance, their dishonesty, their wastefulness, and the like. The economic failure of recipients is more likely to be viewed in terms of lack of virtue than of accident or economic forces. Even a cursory examination of the numerous welfare stereotypes and exaggerated generalizations circulating in the United States reveals that they are personalized and individualistic.

Data on the association between individual responsibility for poverty and traditional anti-welfarism from the 1969 survey support this line of argument. High scores on the anti-welfare index were strongly correlated with high scores on the individualistic factors index. Conventional anti-welfarism was also significantly, but inversely, related to structuralism. The higher the score on the structural-factors index, the less likely a respondent was to score high on the anti-welfare index. Moreover, in a recent Boston study a researcher found a strong relationship between adherence to general work ethic tenets and a negative response to the idea of increasing welfare benefits; here too the association between the work ethic and a negative reaction to welfare recipients seemed conspicuous.[64]

THE FUNCTIONS AND CONSEQUENCES OF ANTI-POOR VIEWS

Given the strength and pervasiveness of these critical views, a question arises as to the functions or consequences of both the traditional anti-welfare sentiment and the traditional view of the poor imbedded in the individualistic ethic. What do these beliefs accomplish? What have been their consequences for this society in the past and in the present? Anti-welfarism and anti-poor attitudes among large numbers of Americans in various income classes may be a sign of a lack of awareness of basic economic interests. Anti-poor and other individualistic views offer a distorted mental picture of the social and economic world that has long buttressed the structure of economic inequality.

Historically, as Max Weber and other scholars have pointed out, the individualistic ethic has contributed to the development of Western capitalism. Others have emphasized the impact of capitalism on the ethic. In any event, culturally ingrained exhortations to hard work—seen as leading toward material success—have been particularly important in stimulating the work effort and individualistic life necessary for Western economic development. One indication of poorly developed awareness of class exploitation can be seen in the dominant individualistic focus on personal success. The emphasis on success, opportunity, and mobility has done much to keep the attention of workers "on their own prospects and those of their children." [65] Attention is focused on signs of individual success—which often take the form of private property (for example, house and car)—rather than on the exploitation of all workers by the rich elites. Moreover, the view of poverty as reflecting indolence and immorality has been a strong motivating force behind the hard work of the average worker in capitalist countries. The fear of falling into material poverty was twice buttressed, once by the specter of economic deprivation itself and again by the shame and stigma that such economic deprivation would bring. In the past and the present anti-poor views have played a role in reinforcing the work effort of ordinary workers.

A second and related consequence of anti-poor perspectives among workers has been to focus hostility and discussion on those below, so much so that accusations of immorality and denials of proper work attitudes direct attention away from one's own economic problems and from one's own exploitation by higher-income classes. Schorr, grappling with the level of hostility expressed by many against welfare recipients, argues that the relatively harsh public attacks on, and treatment of, these recipients can be explained in terms of scapegoat theory.[66] Under tension, particularly recurrent economic tension, Americans have selected this disadvantaged group to receive their concentrated hostility, freeing most of them to deal with each other in more relaxed fashion. This scapegoating process also takes the heat off the status quo—off the structure of inequality detrimental even to the lives of middle-income workers, but beneficial to the wealthy ruling elites. By this means, anti-poor sentiments help legitimize the existing class structure. Welfare and other government expenditures for the "immoral" poor and the high taxes they allegedly require are thus seen as a conspicuous and much-discussed public burden, while the much higher proportion of taxes going for such things as military expenditures or for business subsidies receives less attention. Anti-poor views depoliticize the society and forestall conflict by concentrating the attention of workers on the poor at the bottom, diverting the animosity of the bulk of workers downward rather than upward.[67]

The emphasis on individual success and anti-poor views works to separate workers from one another by reinforcing the divisive status lines between workers. Such views retard joint action by all levels of poor and middle-income workers toward collective ends, particularly toward goals of significant social change. Thus the development of a vigorous anti-welfare ideology has diverted the attention of the middle-income workers from their own inequality to the status differences between themselves and poor recipients of public aid (also workers in the past), preventing them from joining together with the very poor in large-scale protest efforts. "People who cannot work toward the same end are ineffective. Their impotence reinforces the status quo." [68] The general work ethic also has the same effect, because an emphasis on competition among individuals contributes to the inability to work collectively for major economic change. "Present competitiveness is counterrevolutionary, designed to keep the existing order in place by reinforcing attitudes and behavior that will accomplish that end." [69]

Yet another consequence of strong anti-welfarism and anti-poor attitudes is reflected in the apparent public tendency to resist evidence to the contrary and to remain in general ignorance about the poor. In a pilot study in a city in central Texas we found a strong reluctance among average citizens to change their misconceptions about welfare, even when contrary evidence was directly presented to them in an interview setting. We also found substantial ignorance in regard to the details of public assistance programs. Most respondents had heard some recent discussion of welfare, but over half admitted they did not know much about the operation of actual welfare programs. [70]

What seems to characterize the majority of rank-and-file Americans, thus, is a significant degree of false consciousness, a striking focus on diversionary issues coupled with a relatively weak consciousness of their own class interests and their own economic oppression. Even many poor workers hold to individualistic perspectives. These diversionary beliefs include the complex set of misconceptions held about poverty and welfare, those myths and exaggerated generalizations which indicate a distorted view of the economic world. This is an important part of what Anderson has termed the "bourgeois world view." He argues that "to persist in the bourgeois world view at a time when the contradictions between the forces and relations of production are growing is to have a distorted mental picture of reality, to have false consciousness." [71] Yet false consciousness is not an "all-or-nothing phenomenon." Many workers reflect some mixed feelings about the poor; most also have some awareness of the role the capitalists ("bosses") play in their own economic problems—an awareness that has fluctuated significantly with economic changes such as those manifest in the Great Depression of the 1930s. Pragmatic acceptance of modest reforms from time to time is indicative of this. Whether the current low level of class consciousness among workers will be altered by the serious economic difficulties facing workers in the United States in the mid-1970s yet remains to be seen.

Obviously, in addition to their consequences for the relationship between workers and the governing elites, anti-poor attitudes have had a direct and indirect impact on the welfare system in the United States. The impact results from the constant reiteration of the ideology of anti-welfarism and the broader ideology of individualism. Such views reinforce the overt and covert purposes of the existing welfare system. Attempts to reform the morals of the poor receive public support here, as do attempts to maximize the work effort of the poor whatever the cost to the poor. And the dogged persistence of this attitude has been one significant factor shaping legislative and administrative restrictiveness in regard to welfare programs, payments, and regulations. Doubtless many legislators and other elected officials at the various levels of government, particularly local and state levels, have been influenced by negative public views of the poor and of welfare recipients; perhaps more important, they have long shaped public views of the poor and of welfare in speeches, in policy-making activity, and in building basic welfare arrangements. There has long been a reciprocal relationship. In addition, occasional deviations from traditional approaches by liberal officials have been generally restrained by the persisting ideology.

IDEOLOGICAL REPRESSION

Have average Americans come to these anti-poor views in a vacuum? What reinforces the false consciousness of many ordinary Americans? Why do most workers remain rather conservative ideologically? Who benefits the most from individualism? It seems that the individualistic ethic has been carefully taught to most Americans over the course of their lives. This ideology and its associated beliefs—such beliefs as those about welfare, private property, and free enterprise—have been vigorously propagated by Western leaders for several centuries. Protestant leaders early espoused these perspectives. With the acceleration of Western capitalism in the nineteenth century the ruling elites reinforced the ideology of individualism and propagated it aggressively throughout the population. They were "largely successful in establishing the competitive individualist world view and ideology throughout all classes of the society." [72] Beliefs justifying this new economic system were the ruling ideas, and they came to appear more and more as part of the natural order of things. While those in the most advantaged classes have vigorously supported the ideology of individualism, majorities of other income groups have long been persuaded by much of it as well. Once the beliefs became dominant, they had an inertia of their own.

Wolfe has argued suggestively that this situation can be viewed in terms of ideological repression: "The goal of ideological repression now is to win support for the capitalist system, not for any one of its policies." [73] Dominant beliefs and ideas have not come to dominate magically. They have been "consciously and subconsciously disseminated through the means of mental production, i.e., the press, the schools, the churches, the state, etc." [74] Some private organizations, such as advertising agencies and the mass media, have routinely reinforced prevailing ideologies. Periodic advertising campaigns on productivity and the need for greater work effort, as well as routine accents on individualism and competitiveness, illustrate the importance of this sector. A major function of advertising is to maintain allegiance to the American system and its core values. A variety of television programs also reinforce competitive and individualistic values from an early age. Various newspaper and book publications further circulate dominant values, as do private associations such as veterans' groups and union groups.

Public ideological repression is also of importance. State propaganda operations have long been very important in propagating the individualistic ethic. News releases and speeches by elected officials at the various levels of government have circulated much propaganda not only about individualism and competition but also about welfare and the poor. From time to time in the last few years, a few officials in federal welfare agencies have tried to counteract poverty and welfare stereotypes by issuing various research reports or by public comments, but their counterattacks have not offset the dominant views. The public educational system, as well, has played an important role in indoctrinating basic work ethic values in successive generations of young Americans.

Private and public ideological repression do not always have to be conscious. "What makes indoctrination and manipulation in democratic societies so interesting is that they are very often voluntary, haphazard, and even unconscious." [75] Many organizations do not have ideological repression as a central function; it is a side effect. Once the ethic of individualism became part and parcel of the institutions of this society, its propagation became part of the normal operation of those institutions. As with objects, ideologies seem to have their own laws of inertia. Once set into motion, they tend to persist. Particularly important too is a kind of self-repression among ordinary citizens whereby those who have gained economically—no matter how small the gain may be—vigorously support dominant individualistic views out of fear of losing what they have gained. The counter-ideologies that are circulated in the mass media and elsewhere from time to time are resisted out of concern, conscious or unconscious, that attempts to replace the dominant individualism and its system might lead to losing what one has. Reinforcement of individualistic values has not always been completely consistent, but the various factors in the process have contributed to the hardy persistence of individualism. Moreover, acceptance of modest reforms benefiting some working-class or middle-income groups does not require acceptance of competing counter-ideologies, nor does it even require acceptance of significant reforms benefiting the very poor.

CONCLUSION

In his historical study of poverty issues Bremner concludes that by 1900 the individualistic view of the poor, persisting from earlier times, had become ever more vigorous under the auspices of a rapidly industrializing capitalism. Poverty was seen as unnecessary but inevitable because of the varying virtue and character of individual Americans.

Taken as a whole, our recent survey data show that such a

critical view of the poor, and particularly the welfare poor, is still prevalent in the United States. In interpreting the causes of poverty and the problems of welfare, Americans still place greater emphasis on individualistic explanations than on structural or fatalistic explanations. Although these data suggest that the structural interpretation has some support, it is clear that the individualistic view is firmly entrenched. This individualism seems particularly characteristic of dominant white groups. Certain minorities, on the other hand, appear to be strongholds of structuralist opinions.

The extent to which public views of the poor may be changing in the structural direction has yet to be determined. It appears that this orientation has become more significant in recent years, and that some people may now be mixing individualistic and structural views in an apparently inconsistent fashion. Whether this is a major trend is yet an open question. Nevertheless, as long as the tendency of Americans to individualize their economic and social problems persists, attempts at redistributive reform in economic and political areas—for the poor and middle-income groups—would seem to be out of the question. As we have suggested previously, individualistic interpretations reflect false consciousness and mesh well with establishment attempts to maintain the status quo, whereas structural interpretations lend themselves to attempts at counter-ideologies and at structural reforms in this society. These issues will be further explored in the next chapter.

1. See Harold L. Wilensky and Charles N. Lebeaux, *Industrial Society and Social Welfare* (New York: Free Press, 1965), pp. 34–35; and Robin M. Williams, Jr., *American Society*, 3rd ed. (New York: Alfred A. Knopf, 1970), pp. 454–61.

2. It is not the purpose of this chapter to explore general critiques of the ideology of individualism that suggest that it is being replaced by an organizational or security ethnic. For this perspective, see William H. Whyte, Sr., *The Organization Man* (Garden City, N.Y.: Doubleday Anchor Books, 1956).

3. Robert H. Bremner, *From the Depths* (New York: New York University Press, 1956), pp. 16–17. Bremner also demonstrates that some in the nineteenth century were concerned with the structural origins of poverty, although they were a small minority.

4. Robin M. Williams, Jr., *American Society* (New York: Alfred A. Knopf, 1970), p. 456.

5. The survey was supported by an NIMH Applied Research Branch research

grant (MH15917); field interviews were conducted by the Opinion Research Corporation (Princeton, N.J.) in the spring of 1969. Examination of sample distributions on sex, race, income, region, and city size against U.S. Bureau of the Census figures revealed a close fit; the sample is quite representative of the adult American population in 1969.

6. Wilensky and Lebeaux, *Industrial Society and Social Welfare*, p. 35.

7. The validity of these three indexes can be seen (1) in their face validity and (2) in the positive intercorrelations of the items. Item-to-item (gamma) associations ranged as follows: (1) individualistic-factors index, $+.43$ to $+.59$ ($x = +.51$); (2) structural-factors index, $+.27$ to $+.61$ ($x = +.41$); (3) fatalistic-factors index, $+.08$ to $+.38$ ($x = +.25$). The weakest case for validity is in regard to the fatalistic-factors index, because of the somewhat weaker face validity and the lower item-to-item correlations. The only association not reaching the level of at least $+.27$ was that between item 3 and item 11; however, because item 3 correlated well with item 5 on the same index, it was decided to include it in the index for the purposes of further analysis. However, this variation emphasizes the exploratory nature of the indexes.

8. Max Weber, *The Protestant Ethic and the Spirit of Capitalism*, transl. Talcott Parsons (New York: Charles Scribner's Sons, 1958).

9. Gerhard Lenski, *The Religious Factor*, rev. ed. (New York: Doubleday Anchor Books, 1963).

10. Joan Huber and William H. Form, *Income and Ideology* (New York: Free Press, 1973), pp. 101 ff.

11. Edgar May, *The Wasted Americans* (New York: Signet Books, 1964), p. 13.

12. In 1969 we drew on an unpublished paper, a revised revision of which was subsequently published. See David J. Kallen and Dorothy Miller, "Public Attitudes toward Welfare," *Social Work*, 16 (July 1971), 83–90.

In our interview schedule four statements are phrased in the anti-welfare direction, agreement with which indicates a negative assessment of welfare recipients (1, 2, 3, 7); three are stated in the favorable direction, agreement with which generally indicates a favorable or sympathetic view of welfare recipients (4, 5, 6). Item 4 deals with programs rather than people on welfare, but reflects a position often taken by those who have a sympathetic view of the plight of welfare recipients. For our purposes here, respondents disagreeing with these favorable items are generally considered to be anti-welfare—unsympathetic to those on welfare.

13. Social and Rehabilitation Service, U.S. Department of Health, Education and Welfare, *Public Assistance Statistics*: November 1969 (Washington, D.C.: National Center for Social Statistics, 1969).

14. Los Angeles County Bureau of Public Assistance, *A Look at a Welfare Family in Los Angeles* (Los Angeles, California, 1966); Robert C. Stone and Fredric T. Schlamp, *Family Life Styles below the Poverty Line* (San Francisco, Cal.: Institute for Social Science Research, San Francisco State College, 1966); Social and Rehabilitation Service, U.S. Department of Health, Education and Welfare, *Welfare Myths vs. Facts* (Washington, D.C.: U.S. Government Printing Office, 1971).

15. Social and Rehabilitation Service, *Welfare Myths vs. Facts.*

16. John B. Williamson, "Beliefs about the Welfare Poor," Unpublished paper, Boston College, Chestnut Hill, Massachusetts, 1974.

17. Reported in a personal letter (with statistical enclosures) to the author from James L. Costa, Commissioner, Assistance Payments Administration, dated June 3, 1970.

18. Bradley R. Schiller, "Empirical Studies of Welfare Dependency: A Survey," *The Journal of Human Resources*, 8 (Supplement, 1973), 25.

19. *Ibid.*, p. 21.

20. Samuel M. Meyers and Jennie McIntyre, *Welfare Policy and Its Consequences for the Recipient Population: A Study of the AFDC Program* (Washington, D.C.: U.S. Government Printing Office, 1969).

21. Lawrence Podell, *Families on Welfare in New York City* (New York: The Center for the Study of Urban Problems, The City University of New York, n.d.).

22. Schiller, "Empirical Studies of Welfare Dependency," p. 22.

23. Leonard Goodwin, *Do the Poor Want to Work?* (Washington, D.C.: The Brookings Institution, 1972), p. 112.

24. *Ibid.*, p. 113.

25. Martin Warren and Sheldon Berkowitz, "The Employability of AFDC Mothers and Fathers," *Welfare in Review*, 7 (July–August 1969), 1–7. See also Harold Yahr and Richard Pomeroy, *Studies in Public Welfare: Effects of Eligibility Investigation on Welfare Clients* (New York: The Center for the Study of Urban Problems, The City University of New York, 1969).

26. Podell, *Families on Welfare in New York City.*

27. Williamson, "Beliefs about the Welfare Poor."

28. U.S. Department of Health, Education and Welfare, *Eligibility of Families Receiving Aid to Families with Dependent Children: January–April, 1963* (Washington, D.C.: U.S. Government Printing Office, 1963).

29. Social and Rehabilitation Service, U.S. Department of Health, Education and Welfare, *Developments in Dealing with Questions of Recipient Fraud in Public Assistance: 1951–1967* (Washington, D.C.: National Center for Social Statistics, 1969).

30. U.S. Department of Health, Education and Welfare, *HEW News* (January 1972). This same report found a significant proportion of clients receiving overpayments or underpayments, most often because of agency error, although client errors were also important. That there are some serious administrative problems in the current welfare system is not to be denied; but ineligibility and errors do not necessarily add up to recipient fraud.

31. *Ibid.*

32. *Ibid.;* see also Los Angeles, County Bureau of Public Assistance, *A Look at a Welfare Family in Los Angeles;* Utah State Department of Public Welfare, Facts about People on Welfare in Utah (Utah, 1967); Social and Rehabilitation Service, *Developments in Dealing with Questions of Recipient Fraud in Public Assistance.*

33. Meyers and McIntyre, *Welfare Policy.*

34. Citizen's Committee for Children of New York, *Public Welfare: Myth vs. Fact* (New York, 1963).

35. Social and Rehabilitation Service, U.S. Department of Health, Education and Welfare, *Preliminary Report of Findings: 1969 AFDC Study* (Washington, D.C.: National Center for Social Statistics, 1970). Although it may come as a surprise to some, illegitimacy figures were *lower* in some Deep South states than in the North. Georgia, for example, reported an illegitimacy figure of 17 percent.

36. Social and Rehabilitation Service, *Welfare Myths vs. Facts.*

37. *ReStat Report*, Division of Welfare, Utah State Department of Health and Welfare, 1969; see also Social and Rehabilitation Service, *Welfare Myths vs. Facts.*

38. Social and Rehabilitation Service, *Welfare Myths vs. Facts.* See also *Public Welfare: Myth vs. Fact.*

39. Utah State Department of Health and Welfare, *Facts about People on Welfare in Utah.*

40. Meyers and McIntyre, *Welfare Policy.*

41. The HEW report is cited in Williamson, "Beliefs about the Welfare Poor"; see also Social and Rehabilitation Service, *Welfare Myths vs. Facts.*

42. "About Public Aid: Comments and Clarifications," *Public Aid in Illinois* (March 1970), pp. 2–10.

43. Social and Rehabilitation Service, *Preliminary Report of Findings.*

44. "About Public Aid: Comments and Clarifications," *Public Aid in Illinois.*

45. Charles Tilly, "Race and Migration to the American City," in *The Urban Scene*, ed. Joe R. Feagin (New York: Random House, 1973), pp. 38–39.

46. *Ibid.*, p. 39.

47. William L. Hamilton, Frederick C. Collignon, and Carol E. Carlson, *The Causes of Rural to Urban Migration among the Poor* (Cambridge, Mass.: Abt Associates, Inc., 1970), p. 19.

48. See Daniel O. Price, *A Study of Economic Consequences of Rural to Urban Migration* (Austin, Texas: Tracor, 1969); Gene B. Petersen and Laure M. Sharp, *Southern Migrants to Cleveland* (Washington, D.C.: Bureau of Social Science Research, Inc., 1969).

49. Larry H. Long, "Poverty Status and Receipt of Welfare among Migrants and Nonmigrants in Large Cities," paper presented at the annual meeting of the Population Association of America, New Orleans, Louisiana, April 26–28, 1973.

50. The same is true of the aggregate demographic studies that have tried to correlate welfare payment levels with general migration data. The results here are inconclusive in part because of the aggregate level of analysis. See Gordon F. DeJong and William L. Donnelly, "Public Welfare and Migration," *Social Science Quarterly*, 54 (September 1973), 329–44.

51. *The Boston Sunday Globe*, July 21, 1970, p. 47.

52. Total income is also low. Income, in addition to welfare payments, averaged $50 a month for AFDC families in the 1967 study, with even smaller amounts for other welfare recipients. Social and Rehabilitation Service, U.S. Department of Health, Education and Welfare, *1967 AFDC Study: Preliminary Report of Findings from*

Mail Questionnaire (Washington, D.C.: National Center for Social Statistics, 1969).

53. Social and Rehabilitation Service, *Welfare Myths vs. Facts*.

54. In the last two years this multiple-benefit issue has received some attention in congressional discussions and investigations, but it has been greatly exaggerated. See U.S. Congress, Joint Economic Committee, *Studies in Public Welfare*, Paper No. 1, *Public Income Transfer Programs: The Incidence of Multiple Benefits and the Issues Raised by their Receipt* (Washington, D.C.: U.S. Government Printing Office, 1972).

55. Social and Rehabilitation Service, *1967 AFDC Study: Preliminary Report of Findings from Mail Questionnaire*.

56. For a hard-hitting defense of this point by a welfare recipient organization, see National Welfare Rights Organization, *Six Myths about Welfare* (Washington, D.C., 1971), pp. 8–9.

57. California State Department of Social Welfare, *Why Welfare in California?* (Sacramento, Cal., 1966). One welfare budget in the mid-1960s was $891 million, 44 percent of which was contributed by the federal government and 40 percent by state government.

58. See Social and Rehabilitation Service, *Welfare Myths vs. Facts*; National Welfare Rights Organization, *Six Myths about Welfare*.

59. Disagreement with an item stated in a direction indicating sympathy for welfare recipients was scored as a *traditional* anti-welfare response for the purpose of creating the anti-welfare index.

60. Williamson, "Beliefs about the Welfare Poor."

61. Kallen and Miller, "Public Attitudes toward Welfare," p. 88.

62. *Ibid.*, pp. 89–90. See also May, *The Wasted Americans*, p. 38.

63. Bernard L. Diamond, "The Children of Leviathan," *California Law Review*, 54, May 1966, 357–69.

64. Williamson, "Beliefs about the Welfare Poor."

65. Charles H. Anderson, *Toward a New Sociology*, rev. ed. (Homewood, Ill.: Dorsey Press, 1974), p. 125.

66. Alvin L. Schorr, "Problems in the ADC Program," unpublished paper in author's possession, n.d.

67. See Richard C. Edwards, "Who Fares Well in the Welfare State?" in *The Capitalist System*, ed. Richard C. Edwards et al. (Englewood Cliffs, N.J.: Prentice-Hall, Inc., 1972), p. 250.

68. Alan Wolfe, *The Seamy Side of Democracy* (New York: David McKay Co., 1973), p. 136.

69. *Ibid.*, p. 137.

70. This study was conducted with Claudia Rappaport in the Austin, Texas area.

71. Charles H. Anderson, *The Political Economy of Social Class* (Englewood Cliffs, N.J.: Prentice-Hall, Inc., 1974), p. 60.

72. *Ibid.*

73. Wolfe, *The Seamy Side of Democracy*, p. 133. His italics have been omitted.

74. Anderson, *The Political Economy of Social Class*, p. 60.

75. Wolfe, *The Seamy Side of Democracy*, p. 171.

5

Public Aid for the Poor: New Approaches

Since the 1930s a major government strategy for dealing with the public assistance system has been to tinker with that system in order to alter or improve its operation. This tinkering can be seen in the movement from more, to less, to more local control, and in the shift to a services strategy in the early 1960s and then to a work-oriented strategy in the late 1960s. As we noted in Chapter 3, a number of important external determinants play a role in shaping the welfare system, most of which have operated in a way that accepts the existing system as a given. We have also noted the variety of governing class and work ethic goals imbedded in public relief for the poor, as well as the often negative attitudes of the average citizen in regard to welfare.

Not surprisingly, then, in the last decade or two some critics of the existing welfare system have called for its replacement by a new approach, the exact character of which varies with the critic. Most critics have had in mind the public welfare system, although it is clear that most have also been concerned with another large category, loosely termed "the working poor." By this term is meant those poor families with part-time or full-time, and usually male, workers who do not presently qualify for cash assistance. So the new approaches, while usually encompassing recipients of traditional welfare aid, have often had a broader public in mind: most poor people below a certain level of income. It is also important to note that some new proposals, though they are often seen as alternatives to welfare, are in fact only partial alternatives, because they might not benefit all the welfare poor.

A variety of new approaches to the problems of welfare and poverty have been devised—the guaranteed annual income plan, the negative income tax, the family allowance, the guaranteed job approach. It is one purpose of this concluding chapter to review some of the more prominent new proposals of alternatives to the existing welfare system. But first we will examine public opinion on eradicating poverty in the United States to provide part of the attitudinal context for a discussion of alternatives.

VIEWS ON PUBLIC ACTION

As we have seen, American views on the poor are often inconsistent. In some ways public attitudes are a "mixed bag," for strong negative attitudes toward the poor or welfare recipients on many issues can co-exist with more positive assessments on other issues. Although the dominant tone for a given individual may be critical and greatly influenced by the individualistic ideology, in numerous cases a secondary theme reflects some sympathy for the poor. Moreover, in the national sample interviewed in 1969, we found important minorities of Americans who deviated significantly from conventional anti-welfare and anti-poor sentiment in the direction of -emphasizing flaws in the structure of the economic system. Thus it is not surprising that opinions on what to do about the poor also seem to be inconsistent.

A major objective of the 1969 survey—and of a 1972 follow-up survey independently conducted by the Opinion Research Corporation (ORC)—was to examine public views on strategies for dealing with poverty, including views on some relatively new strategies that have been advocated in recent years.[1] On the one hand, most Americans seem pessimistic about the complete eradication of poverty in the United States. In both the 1969 and 1972 surveys we asked a straightforward question: "Do you think poverty will ever be done away with in this country, or not?" Eighty percent answered in the negative, and another 10 percent expressed uncertainty. Doubtless, this perspective has been greatly influenced by the pervasive and ancient Christian view that "the poor you shall always have with you."

On the other hand, although most respondents were pessimistic about the present or future eradication of poverty, most still felt that some attempt should be made. Thus in response to a question about an "all-out effort by the federal government to get rid of poverty," 73 percent gave a generally favorable response in the 1969 survey. By 1972 the proportion viewing such a federal effort favorably had climbed to 78 percent. Americans, traditionally pragmatic and action-oriented, seem unwilling to ignore the problem of poverty. Of course, these general responses say nothing about the specific type of government response desired. Many respondents may be thinking in terms of accentuated but traditional welfare programs, or of doing something in regard to work requirements, or they may simply believe that something, left unspecified even in their own minds, *must* be done.

What about the involvement of the private sector in dealing with poverty in the United States? If given the chance, would most respondents choose private industry solutions over government solutions? Republican leaders have traditionally urged private business and industry to assume a primary role in dealing with poverty, while Democratic leaders have seen the goal as a cooperative government-industry effort. When the nationwide sample was asked in 1969 whether private industry or the federal government should be mainly responsible for anti-poverty programs, 12 percent favored private industry acting alone, and another 34 percent saw both acting together as the correct approach. Forty-one percent felt that the federal government should be mainly responsible. The rest were uncertain or gave other answers. More recently, a 1972 ORC survey asked the same question and found little change in the pattern of responses. There was a small change in the proportion favoring joint action by private industry and the government—up from 34 percent to 39 percent. Again, we see that the exact character of the government and private action to be taken to deal with poverty remains unspecified.

POSSIBLE ALTERNATIVES TO WELFARE
AND POVERTY PROGRAMS

Because we were interested in the national concern with public alternatives to welfare that had surfaced in the mid-1960s, we asked the respondents to the 1969 nationwide sample how they felt about three proposals that have been suggested as partial or total alternatives to existing welfare and poverty programs. In addition, some of these new proposals would aid many of the so-called "working poor," as well as the unemployed poor and those receiving public assistance. The proposals offered for the respondents to assess were: a job-guarantee program, an income-guarantee proposal, and a more radical equal-income proposal. Two would involve cash in a direct way, while the job-guarantee proposal indirectly would provide cash aid. Specific proposals for government action in recent years have taken the form of guaranteed-job and guaranteed-income proposals, which we will now examine.

A GUARANTEED-JOB PROPOSAL

At first, a majority of the respondents seemed to favor a job-guarantee proposal. The proposal, seen by some analysts as a partial solution to welfare and poverty problems, was phrased thus: "Some people have proposed that the federal government guarantee a job to every American who wants to work even if it means creating a lot of public jobs like during the Depression."

Percentage of Respondents

Favor	64%	
(Favor with higher taxes)		35%
Oppose	26	
Can't say/other	10	
	100%	

Nearly two-thirds of the respondents initially said they would favor "workfare"; the impact of the work ethic seems clear in these responses. But that group was reduced almost by half when a follow-up question measuring the degree of commitment to the plan was presented. When asked if they would still favor the job-guarantee program even if it meant a significant increase in their own taxes, only half of those initially in favor replied "yes." This proportion works out to about one-third of the total sample favoring the federal job-guarantee plan with higher personal taxes. Workfare, yes! Workfare with higher taxes, no!

A GUARANTEED-INCOME PLAN

An income-guarantee plan for families fared even worse. In reply to a question dealing with a federal government guaranteed (minimum) income of about $3,000 for every American family ("instead of providing welfare and relief payments"), 61 percent of the sample indicated that they were *opposed* to such a guarantee, even though the income specified would be considered by federal analysts, and by these respondents as well, as below the poverty line for average-sized families.

Percentage of Respondents

Favor income guarantee	30%
Oppose income guarantee	61
Can't say/other	10
	101% *

* Some totals do not add up to 100 percent because of rounding procedures.

Only 30 percent were unequivocally in favor of such a guarantee; the rest were uncertain or gave a miscellaneous assortment of answers. No follow-up question testing degree of commitment was asked in this case, but it is likely that a question indicating the tax costs of such a plan would have reduced support for this proposal to a small minority of the sample. Those who opposed the idea of a guaranteed income most frequently explained their responses in individualistic terms (fear that people would stop working, not work very hard, become government dependents, lose ambition or motivation, or waste the money), or simply stated that they were opposed to "handouts" and "giveaways." The influence of the ideology of individualism again seems clear. Only about 9 percent of the total sample were opposed because they either felt the level was too low or that such a program should be handled by agencies other than the federal government. It is interesting that this proposal was rejected by the majority of Americans just a few months before President Richard M. Nixon introduced a more restricted version of this same income-guarantee approach.

SOME TRENDS

The 1972 follow-up survey by the Opinion Research Corporation found that support for both the guaranteed-job and guaranteed-income approaches had increased somewhat.

Percentage of Respondents in Favor

	1969		1972	
Guaranteed-job plan	64%		72%	
(with higher taxes)		35%		42%
Guaranteed-income plan	30		38	

Those favoring the job-guarantee approach increased to nearly three-quarters from 1969 to 1972, while those who favored it even if it meant higher taxes increased to 42 percent. Those who favored the guaranteed income increased to 38 percent, perhaps influenced by the events of the intervening years. Perhaps most important, a substantial majority of the sample was still opposed to or uncertain about both these proposals. Even the workfare proposal still could not generate majority support in 1972, if the plan would involve increased taxes. However, commitment to workfare remained stronger than to a guaranteed-income plan, revealing the continuing strength of the work ethic. It is important to remember that support is probably being expressed here for guaranteeing jobs to those who want to work.

EQUALIZING INCOME

The most radical proposal—substantial income redistribution—was overwhelmingly vetoed by the nationwide sample in the 1969 survey. The question came right after the other redistributive plans and was phrased in terms of equalizing family incomes, but was not as carefully spelled out as it might have been. The suggestion that "every family in this country should receive the same income, about $10,000 or so" was opposed by no less than 80 percent of the total sample. Thirteen percent favored it; the rest were uncertain. Those few who favored this somewhat vague proposal generally explained their answers in egalitarian terms, such as "things should be more equal," "people could live better," or "it would curb poverty and reduce its harmful effects."

	Percentage of Respondents
Favor equal income	13%
Oppose equal income	80
Can't say/other	7
	100%

Proponents and opponents seemed to view this proposal as a way of dealing with poverty and with inequality. Those who opposed a relatively equal income distribution talked primarily in terms of traditional individualistic and work ethic perspectives, citing most frequently such things as "people should work for a living," "it makes no allowances for differences in ability," "people should get what they work for," "it would be communistic," and related responses. Opposition seemed to be intense, and few opposed it because they wanted an even more radical plan or a higher income level. It might well be that a few more respondents would have supported this relatively radical redistributive proposal had it been phrased explicitly in terms of work or holding a job, but that remains an open question. Although the question did not specifically mention government involvement in the equalizing process, most respondents seemed to assume that such involvement would be required. This was clearly a reasonable assumption.

SOCIAL CORRELATES

Is support for these proposals, which are seen by some as new approaches to public aid for the poor, randomly distributed throughout the population? Who supports them? Table 5 summarizes the patterns of support. Will those socioreligious groups which are the most individualistic in their general orientation toward the poor be the least likely to support new plans that might improve the conditions of the poor? As we have noted previously, some scholars have argued that government-intervention solutions to economic problems should receive the least support in those groups, such as white Protestants, most firmly tied to economic individualism.

In the 1969 survey the greatest support for a federal guaranteed-job plan came from those groups with the least commitment to the individualistic interpretation of poverty and the greatest commitment to the structural interpretation—black Protestants and Jews, with 83 percent and 73 percent in favor, respectively. Less impressive majorities of the white Protestants and Catholics favored this governmental solution (without the increased taxes proviso). When an even more controversial program—the guaranteed-income proposal—was suggested, the pattern of support was roughly similar to that for the job-guarantee program. Fifty-nine percent of the black Protestants were in favor of such an alternative to welfare, followed by just under half of the Jews and only a quarter of the other whites. In this case, the difference between white Catholics and white Protestants was negligible. The most radical proposal of all, distribution of income so that every family

TABLE 5
SUPPORT FOR NEW PROPOSALS,
BY DEMOGRAPHIC SUBGROUPS (1969 SURVEY)

	Proportion in Favor		
	Guaranteed-Job Plan	Guaranteed-Income Plan	Equal-Income Plan
Socioreligious Group			
white Protestant (*N* =542)	58%	25%	9%
white Catholic (*N* = 218)	67	26	17
black Protestant (*N* = 110)	83	59	25
Jewish (*N* = 26)	73	46	4
Racial Group			
white (*N* = 839)	61	26	11
black (*N* = 122)	84	57	27
other nonwhite (*N* = 47)	79	32	22
Region			
Northeast (*N* = 247)	71	29	16
North Central (*N* = 289)	57	24	14
South (*N* = 297)	66	34	13
West (*N* = 182)	64	37	8
Age			
under 30 (*N* = 232)	66	35	11
30–49 (*N* = 378)	66	29	15
50 + (*N* = 405)	62	29	13
Family Income			
under $4,000 (*N* = 279)	69	39	14
$4,000–5,999 (*N* = 155)	68	30	17
$6,000–9,999 (*N* = 283)	66	30	16
$10,000 or more (*N* = 285)	57	23	7
Education			
6th grade or less (*N* = 112)	71	38	24
7th–11th (*N* = 345)	73	36	17
12th grade, technical school (*N* = 322)	63	25	12
some college or more (*N* = 234)	49	25	3

would have about the same, was rejected by large majorities in all socioreligious categories.

As before, racial group was significantly associated with respondent attitudes. Black respondents were much more likely than white respondents to support a job-guarantee program (84 percent versus 61 percent), a guaranteed-income program (57 percent versus 26 percent), and an equal family-income proposal (27 percent versus 11 percent), while the other nonwhites fell between the two larger groups in each case. Note too that a majority of all three groups supported the guaranteed-job plan without the increased taxes proviso, but only a minority in each case applauded the equalized-income proposal.

The regional pattern was not consistent from one proposal to the next. Those in the Northeast region were the most likely to favor the job-guarantee plan and the equal family-income proposal, while those in the West were the most likely to favor the guaranteed-income plan. A majority of the subsamples in all regions supported the job-guarantee plan (without the higher taxes proviso), but only minorities in all regions supported the two income proposals. Moreover, age was not significantly related to any of the new proposals, although in the case of the job- and income-guarantee plans the youngest group (under 30) was a little more likely than the others to be in favor. Note again that a majority of all three age groups favored the job-guarantee plan, but only a minority of each age group expressed approval in regard to the two income proposals.

Income and support for the two less radical proposals were inversely related: the poorer the respondent, the more likely he or she was to support the proposals. The poor (under $4,000), those with the most to gain, were the most likely to approve of such changes, while those in the affluent bracket (over $10,000) were the least likely to approve. Again, however, a majority in all income subgroups supported the work-guarantee plan, but only a minority —including a minority of the low-income respondents—were in favor of the guaranteed-income plans.

Again the liberalizing effect of a college education seemed absent. As formal education increased, support decreased. In each case those with a sixth-grade education or less were the most likely to approve the proposals, while the college-educated were least likely to approve. Support for the guaranteed-job program and guaranteed-income programs significantly decreased with education. Yet even with this variation at least half of all the educational groups supported the job-guarantee approach (without the higher taxes proviso), but only a minority favored the income proposals.

In summary, analysis of background variables revealed that favorability to three proposals was not equally distributed. With a few important exceptions, those groups with the largest proportions *favoring* the three proposals were:

1. Black Protestants and Jews
2. Those in the low-income range
3. Those with the least formal education

Noteworthy for their absence in this list are the dominant white categories.

INDIVIDUALISM AND SUPPORT
FOR NEW PROGRAMS

What is the relationship between general views of the poor and support for these new proposals? Are those whose basic beliefs are most in tune with the traditional individualistic ideology the most likely to reject guaranteed-job or guaranteed-income programs? Are those with strong structure-oriented views more likely to support the new plans? The answer in each case is yes. Survey respondents who scored high on the individualistic-factors index, which was discussed in a previous chapter, were *less likely* than those who scored low to support all the new proposals. The opposite pattern holds for those who emphasized structural and fatalistic factors as very important causes of poverty. Particularly strong is the relationship between scores on the structural-factors index and support for the three programs. Eighty-four percent of those giving *great emphasis* to structural factors in the forces lying behind poverty also *favored* the job-guarantee program, compared to less than half of those regarding such factors as unimportant. Similarly, as one moves from the high to the low categories on the structural-factors index, the proportion favoring the guaranteed-income program drops from just under half to 15 percent, while the proportion favoring the equal-income proposal drops from one-quarter to 8 percent. The pattern is essentially similar in regard to the fatalistic-factors index. Of course, the individualistic-factors index deals with opinions on poverty causes and is not the only measure of individualism. Broader measures, including other aspects of the work ethic not related to the poor, might add to the prediction of opposition to these innovative and redistributive programs.

RULING ELITES AND
ALTERNATIVES TO WELFARE

Public views of new proposals and plans set out as alternatives to existing public assistance and poverty programs constitute important information for understanding the possibility of reform. Not only do programs have economic and social costs, as we will see shortly, but they also have political costs. One of the constraints on governmental action is public opinion, both public beliefs about relatively specific policy proposals and general individualistic beliefs about work and material success. As we have seen, new proposals seen as alternatives to existing aid programs for the poor vary in their degree of acceptability to the general public. So we now have a sense of public attitudes. It seems clear, for example, that a guaranteed-job program would garner more public support in the political process than a large-scale guaranteed-income program.

But public views on poverty and welfare constitute only one of the important constraints on new departures in public policy. At least as important are the views of powerful elite groups and the support such groups present for policy alternatives. Of course, such groups usually share in the work-oriented ideology of individualism, which they have also fostered. But some members of the ruling elites often seem more sensitive to serious problems with the existing political or economic system well before those problems become obvious to the larger population. Thus the primary reason for asking the survey questions on income and job proposals was that these issues were increasingly being discussed by some influential academic, business, and government officials in the 1960s. We will now examine some innovative proposals from these influential groups, keeping in mind the larger ideological context within which they have been offered.

Traditional programs have suffered much criticism for a number of decades, both from members of the governing elite and from the average American. In a previous chapter we examined some of those external determinants which have had an impact on the public assistance structure, particularly on those cash-assistance programs growing out of the 1935 Social Security Act. Indeed, we have seen numerous attempts to tinker with or repair the existing welfare structure. In addition to these attempts at refurbishing the existing system, a number of alternatives to the existing welfare system were being proposed in a forthright way by the late 1960s. By the time of the 1969 survey, among social scientists, liberal and conservative, at prominent universities there was serious debate over programs involving new departures in transferring cash to poor families by the government. Many of those advocating new approaches saw them as at least partial alternatives to the existing welfare system, although many have also been concerned with the larger category of the so-called "working poor." Guaranteed income, negative income tax, job-guarantee plans—these phrases were prominent not only in the vocabularies of academic types but also, by the late 1960s, in the discussions of important economic and political leaders.

The emergence of innovative proposals often reflected a growing concern about the existing system and the "welfare crisis." There was great dissatisfaction over previous attempts at reform. Often cited were arguments about the alleged negative effect of welfare on family stability and about the problems of the millions of poor families who could not qualify for welfare. Concern over the apparent failure of the War on Poverty, with its expansion of training and services programs, was also reflected in the "welfare crisis" debate among influential Americans. Clearly, some of the worry was related to a genuine regard for the suffering of the poor. Perhaps even more important, however, was the growing political protest of the late 1950s and 1960s. New political pressure from blacks, Chicanos, Native Americans, welfare rights groups, and unions of low-wage workers accelerated elite involvement in the development of new strategies to deal with poverty. The basic fabric of the society seemed to be in trouble. What Ozawa has noted for government officials seems to have been true for academic and business leaders as well:

Long ago, American lawmakers resisted helping the poor—not because they hated poor people, but because granting them a decent life hindered rather than contributed to the maintenance of existing social structures. In recent years anti-poverty programs have flourished. This does not mean that Americans suddenly learned the virtues of humanitarianism. It merely reflects the growing realization that guaranteeing minimum standards of living for all is becoming a prerequisite for the nation's survival without a revolution.[2]

Additional stimulus for elite concern over expanded aid to the poor came from those worried about state and local protest over rising taxes, taxes often associated with welfare. Indeed, it was this growing state and local cost that helped fuel talk about a dramatic "welfare crisis." Important too was elite anxiety over the state of the economy. Yet it must be noted that only *some* members of the ruling elites supported innovative departures in public policy.

GUARANTEED-INCOME PROPOSALS

Academic critics of government welfare programs have been in the forefront of those advocating innovative guaranteed-income plans. A few had argued for guaranteed incomes for the poor before the 1960s, but it was not until that decade that such plans were seriously or widely debated. A conservative economist, Milton Friedman, developed a negative income tax plan in the late 1950s, a plan popularized in his influential 1962 book, *Capitalism and Freedom*. Under this plan, poor families (including those with an unemployed father) would receive a government benefit payment called a "negative tax," while those above the poverty line would continue to pay taxes. For those with incomes less than the sum of allowed tax exemptions and deductions, Friedman proposed that the federal government pay 50 percent of the difference between that sum and actual family income. A family of four with no income and $3,000 in exemptions and deductions would thus get a government payment of $1,500. If that same family earned $1,000, it would receive 50 percent of the difference between that $1,000 of earned income and the sum of family exemptions in cash from the government, or in this case $1,000 in public aid.[3]

Discussion of this innovative idea clearly reflected conservative concern with the work incentive and with government interference. Friedman explicitly discussed the work incentive involved in allowing poor families to keep a portion of earnings: "Like any other measures to alleviate poverty, it reduces the incentives of those helped to help themselves, but it does not eliminate that incentive entirely, as a system of supplementing incomes up to some fixed minimum would. An extra dollar earned always means more money available for expenditure." [4] Moreover, in his view the negative income tax plan would save money for nonpoor taxpayers, because it would be less costly than the current "rag-bag" of public welfare programs. The primary motivation behind Friedman's proposal, thus, was the *elimination* of all existing welfare and poverty programs, actions thereby reducing government interference in the lives of individuals. Here is a strong dose of individualistic conservatism. Friedman explicitly rejects the egalitarian position, distinguishing sharply between equality of opportunity and material equality. Material equality must not become the aim of the state. The negative income tax provides only a *minimal* subsistence floor aimed at reducing government intervention, not a goal of income equality. [5]

One of the first to develop a proposal for a more liberal guaranteed income in the early 1960s was Robert Theobald, an economic consultant and lecturer. In *Free Men and Free Markets* he developed an idea which subsequently came to be discussed in a number of important books and academic conferences during the 1960s. [6] What are the important aspects of a guaranteed income? The key is to supply money to the poor. "The first area of agreement is that the initial step on the way to eliminate poverty is to supply money rather than moral uplift, cultural refinements, extended education, retraining programs or makework jobs." [7] Theobald favors making a minimum income a legally guaranteed right. The idea is to establish an income floor, sufficient for living in dignity, below which no individual or family could fall. His plan is more generous than that of Friedman. One thousand dollars a year for each adult plus $600 a year for each child were suggested as feasible minimum levels. Thirty-two hundred dollars for a family of four in 1963 was the estimated total figure for minimum subsistence. Those whose earnings did not reach that level would receive government aid to raise income to that figure. Theobald also provides a premium for earned income—a bonus of 10 percent of earned income added to the government payment—in order to preserve the work incentive.[8]

In the last decade or so Friedman and Theobald have been among the first social scientists to give emphasis to a minimum income. Yet the motivation lying behind these two proposals is considerably different. Friedman is primarily concerned with work effort and the growing threat of federal government intervention in the economy. Thus he sets the minimum level very low and provides for a significant work incentive, out of fear that work effort by the poor will otherwise be reduced. Once in effect, the negative income tax would make it possible to do away with existing government programs for the disadvantaged. Theobald, while he agrees that there is a threat to individual liberty from the growing government bureaucracy, believes that an adequate guaranteed-income plan would move the United States "forward into a new societal order." [9] He has argued for a substantially higher minimum guarantee, and does not believe such a subsistence income scheme would limit the work incentive, because most proposals provide a work premium and because economic motivation is not the only reason people work. But Theobald accentuates the future. A guaranteed income is required because of future accelerating automation, which threatens to increase the number of the poor. The short-run benefits have a conservative appeal, for a guaranteed minimum income can operate to preserve the free market. Yet the long-run problems are at least as important, particularly the economy of the future, in which a guaranteed income will be required at a minimally *adequate* (rather than bare subsistence) level without a job requirement.[10] In a number of ways Theobald's most advanced arguments about a guaranteed income border on a more radical distribution of income, because of his stress on a minimum income figure at some future point that would be higher than what is seen as the subsistence level.

By the mid-1960s James Tobin had become a widely respected advocate of a guaranteed-income plan with a zero-income government payment of $1,600 for a family of four. This payment would be reduced by one-third of a dollar for each dollar earned by the family. The breakeven point would be $4,800 for a family of four. In 1968 Tobin raised his zero-income benefit to $3,200 and suggested a higher discount of 50 percent on additional income earned by the family. Then the breakeven income would be $6,400 for a family of four. Up to $6,400 some benefits would accrue; above that figure taxes would be paid.[11] Like Friedman, Tobin is concerned with problems of poverty and welfare and sees his guaranteed-income proposal as, in part, an alternative to the existing welfare system. In his opinion public assistance has proven inadequate as a way of meeting the needs of the poor; implementation of a guaranteed minimum income of this type could lead to a significant decline in welfare costs. Yet Tobin has argued that Friedman's negative income tax sets too low a minimum and does not deal with employment problems. His plan, consequently, includes a more generous minimum level. His motivation is also different from that of the conservative Friedman, for he is concerned with both employment and income strategies for dealing with poverty.[12] The former strategy involves manpower training, the task of fitting the poor to the market, while the guaranteed-income plan relates to income redistribution. Friedman would not support expanded government programs.

Nonetheless, in a fashion similar to Friedman, Tobin indicates his concern with the work-oriented beliefs of the ideology of individualism. Americans remain "mortally afraid that some potential workers will choose idleness even at the expense of income."[13] He suggests that the "carrot," a guaranteed minimum income, may need to be supplemented with the "stick," a work requirement. One "stick" might be to exclude potential workers in calculating income guarantees. One could also require those on payments to present themselves for work: "The widespread, if largely groundless, fear of freeloading can be met by making part, not all, of the assistance to families conditional on the willingness of employable members to present themselves for work or training, and by providing assistance in a way that rewards self-reliance."[14]

Proposals for a guaranteed income such as these were publicly circulated by leading social scientists and other educators in the mid-1960s. Numerous academic statements on a minimum income were issued; numerous meetings were held. In May 1968 a rather influential proposal—a petition calling on Congress to adopt a national guaranteed-income program—was signed by 1,200 prominent economists.[15] Providing a minimum subsistence income was increasingly supported by liberals in the academic community as a solution to poverty and welfare problems. Yet the costs of such a program were often seen as coming out of future economic growth rather than out of redistributing existing income and wealth.

THE BUSINESS COMMUNITY

At first, minimum-income proposals appear to have been discussed primarily among social scientists and welfare professionals. Soon, however, the business community became involved. Late in 1966 a conference of businessmen was sponsored by the United States Chamber of Commerce to debate various minimum income plans.[16] At this time, the Chamber remained more or less neutral on a guaranteed annual income, but the public forum did air the pros and cons of the issue. No longer could the idea of a guaranteed income be considered strictly academic or utopian thinking; some in the business community were becoming receptive to new approaches. But many questions at the conference concerned the morality of receiving income that was not earned or deserved; individualistic, work-oriented values were in evidence at the conference.

Soon thereafter an important meeting of leading businessmen and industrialists was held at Arden House in New York. In 1967 one hundred executives, primarily from the business and industrial community, were assembled by Governor Nelson Rockefeller to discuss state and national welfare crises. After discussion, a steering committee of prominent businessmen was established to synthesize the results and conduct further study.[17] This committee's report came out in the spring of 1968 and tentatively supported a broad income-maintenance system as a replacement for the existing welfare system. A set of conclusions and recommendations was published, including the following:

1. The present system of public assistance does not work well. It covers only 8-million of the 30-million Americans living in poverty. It is demeaning, inefficient, inadequate, and has so many disincentives built into it that it encourages continued dependency.

2. It should be replaced with an income maintenance system, possibly a negative income tax, which would bring all 30 million Americans up to at least the official Federal poverty line. Such a system should contain strong incentives to work, try to contain regional cost of living differentials, and be administered by the Internal Revenue Service to provide greater administrative efficiency and effectiveness than now exists.[18]

The impact of this report on the business community was not as great as it might have been. However, the influential Committee on Economic Development (CED) was impressed by the Arden House report and convened a national meeting of businessmen, educators, and other leaders in May 1968.[19] Yet the CED did not become actively involved in promoting the guaranteed-income idea because of divided opinion among businessmen on a plan seen by many as a radical policy change. Work incentives and the effect on the economy were of paramount concern. Nonetheless, business involvement did have an important influence on subsequent events leading up to the promotion of the Family Assistance Plan (FAP) by President Richard M. Nixon. This indecisiveness on the part of business leaders made it possible for government officials "to pursue welfare reform with some confidence that there would be business support for the product and that no particular business-sponsored proposal had to be taken into account in the planning process." [20] Of course, by their activity prominent members of the business community had set limits on how far a plan for a guaranteed minimum income plan could go.

GOVERNMENTAL ACTIVITY

By the late 1960s interest in a guaranteed-income plan had also grown within a number of important government agencies. An OEO-sponsored experimental negative income tax experiment was under way in New Jersey by 1968. In May 1968, William F. Ryan, a New York congressman, offered the first income guarantee bill ever introduced in Congress; it had been drafted in the Office of Economic Opportunity.[21] In November 1968 planners at the Department of Health, Education and Welfare spelled out in a memorandum four alternative income-maintenance proposals, one of which was a negative income tax plan. Yet the "lame duck" Johnson Administration was unwilling to press such proposals, a clear signal for some observers that the Democratic party was not going to take the lead in these matters.[22]

After the November 1968 election welfare reform became a major issue for the new administration. The guaranteed-income and negative-income tax strategies had by then been widely discussed among social scientists, businessmen, and government agency officials. A number of the new president's closest advisers were so concerned about public welfare that a pre-inaugural Task Force on Public Welfare was established. However, its report only accented the incremental reforms begun by the previous administration.[23] Soon, the new idea of a guaranteed-income proposal was being seriously discussed at the highest levels of the Nixon Administration, pressed on the president by his advisers. There was much heated discussion, pro and con, within the administration; there were ardent opponents of any minimum-income plan. The opponents stressed the need for a work requirement, which was not in an early draft proposal. They also argued from opinion poll data that the general population was opposed to the idea. (Indeed, our 1969 survey data support this argument.) And many in the administration and in Congress found the new plan difficult to understand.[24]

Businessmen and industrialists were carefully consulted in the process of developing the plan. As a result of a briefing of the Arden House Steering Committee in 1968, this corporation-dominated body expressed enthusiastic support for the measure and promised help in getting it through Congress. "Earlier, Nixon had asked that FAP be checked out with businessmen around the country who had shown some interest in the subject of welfare."[25]

Many months later, in August 1969, Nixon's version of a guaranteed minimum income was introduced to the Congress and to the American people. In his welfare reform message to Congress Nixon argued against a "Welfare State that undermines the incentive of the working man." [26] Expressing the views of the ruling elites and a majority of the American people, he argued that the present welfare system is a failure. His forceful denunciation was the ultimate condemnation of the existing welfare system in the 1960s, even suggesting the familiar stereotypical image of lazy recipients in the context of proposing beneficent reform. Furthermore, he proposed a number of concrete reforms, the most innovative of which was a type of guaranteed-income proposal, carefully termed the "Family Assistance Plan" (FAP) to avoid any suggestion that it was actually a guaranteed income. *"I propose that the Federal government pay a basic income to those American families who cannot care for themselves in whichever State they live."* [27] For a family of four with an income of $720 or less the basic minimum payment would be $1,600 a year. With rising income the cash payment would be substantially reduced. This was often seen as a way of replacing the present welfare system (primarily AFDC) with something more work-oriented and less crisis-ridden. The emphasis was also on supplementing the incomes of those male-headed families in which the husband was unemployed or had a very low-paying job. All payments were to be made on the basis of income certification without demeaning investigations. In addition, all employable persons were to be "required to register for work or job training" and "required to accept that work or training." [28] Social services would be provided to facilitate work. Numerous other work-oriented welfare reforms were also spelled out in the message, some of which could be implemented before FAP would go into effect.

Nixon explicitly rejected the alternatives of further tinkering with the existing public assistance system and of adopting a guaranteed income for everyone. Not surprisingly, "work" was the central word in Nixon's welfare reform message to Congress. The word itself appeared eleven times in the first dozen sentences of the message, together with numerous other references to jobs and employment training. It was from the very beginning a message and a proposal pervaded by the work-oriented ideology of individualism. Indeed, the new system was regarded as providing a much stronger work incentive than the existing welfare system. Nixon underlined the FAP work requirement several times. Payments were to be kept below the subsistence level. No payments were to be provided for those who would not work. "No able-bodied person will have a 'free ride' in a nation that provides opportunity for training and work." [29] Similarly, in Nixon's television speech to the American people great emphasis was placed on work: "Under this proposal, everyone who accepts benefits must also accept work or training, provided suitable jobs are available either locally or at some distance if transportation is provided." [30]

In follow-up explanations of the FAP bill by administration officials, stress was placed on the ability of the new program to reform welfare, especially by strengthening family life, and on the government's intent to provide fiscal relief for troubled states. It would ease the tax burden and fiscal crises of localities. Again stressed as an important part of FAP was the combination of work requirements and work incentives. [31] The explicit goals of the Family Assistance Plan reflected concerns not only with the suffering of the poor but also with the problems welfare caused for the governing elite. Of particular concern were the fiscal plight of the states and the work incentive.

Reactions to the Family Assistance Plan, inside and outside the federal government, ranged from strongly positive to strongly negative. The business community was extremely divided on the plan. The national Chamber of Commerce conducted a campaign against FAP, while more liberal businessmen—such as those in the Committee on Economic Development—often favored it. Major voting blocs, both business and labor, also seemed to be divided. [32] A few opinion polls conducted after the president's welfare reform address initially showed a majority of the public favorable to Nixon's articulate call for welfare reform, although it appears that the work emphasis and work requirement aspects of the proposal was what primarily captured the public imagination. "This [public] disposition was abetted by the president's emphasis on work and work training." [33] The very low level of supplementary payments also reduced public opposition, as might be expected. Yet subsequent political events belied this initial optimism about the FAP, for, as was shown in the survey data presented earlier in this chapter, when the cost to the taxpayer became a visible factor, enthusiasm faded significantly. The public was supportive of work-oriented welfare reform but not at its expense.

The Family Assistance Plan passed the House, although there it encountered substantial Southern and conservative opposition. Moderate and liberal Republicans and Democrats carried the day with an emphasis on such features as the restrictive character (the work requirement) of FAP and on the need to deal with state fiscal problems. The Senate, however, presented a different situation. Opposition to the plan grew. Some business organizations, such as the United States Chamber of Commerce, and conservative journals such as *Human Events* were horrified at the bill's apparent success.[34] Subsequently, the Senate did not pass the bill.

Daniel P. Moynihan, a chief engineer of the FAP proposal, sees the final defeat of the bill as the culmination of a conservative strategy, aided by liberals pressing for a more adequate program. Moynihan has been particularly critical of liberal opposition to the plan, which he saw as a significant *redistributive* innovation in public policy. Yet he has probably exaggerated the redistributive aspect of the rather modest FAP plan. That the plan heavily reflected the ideology of individualism can be seen in Moynihan's own critique of those pressing for more generous (but still modest) minimum levels, such as $5,500 for a family of four:

The demand arose not for guaranteed income but for guaranteed wealth. It began to appear that fundamental reform could become fundamental temptation, specifically that upper-middle-class liberals, having lost a sufficient awareness of the privilege—the singularity—of class position, now proposed privilege for all: an attractive thought, but as unattainable as it is illogical.[35]

This fear of ultimate equality—of "privilege for all"—was an important underlying factor in the death and burial of the Family Assistance Plan. Even some of its strongest supporters seemed fearful that fundamental reform might eventually lead to a significant redistribution of income and wealth. So the minimum income floor of FAP was kept to a level well below the poverty line, with a low overall cost: the "virtue of FAP was that it was small enough to fit into a routine budget." [36] It is noteworthy, moreover, that major tax reform was never seriously considered by the Nixon Administration, though even the limited Family Assistance Plan probably would have entailed some additional tax burden for average Americans, or tax reform aimed at the wealthy, in the near future.

CRITICS OF A GUARANTEED INCOME

We have already noted some criticism of these new cash aid proposals. A number of writers with other alternatives in mind have also directed specific criticisms at the prominent guaranteed-income proposals. Not unexpectedly, some analysts have criticized the varying levels of support in the plans. Thus Vadakin questions the lack of consensus on a minimum guarantee level: "While no one could object to holding differing points of view on this score by the architects of the proposals, ideally, as a logical first step, there ought to be some accepted goal as to the guarantee level that would accord with public consensus—provided the guarantee approach to income maintenance is to be utilized." [37] Perhaps more important, plans such as those of Friedman and of the Nixon Administration have been criticized by the most liberal critics for providing a standard of living for those with modest or no income well below the government's own poverty line. Some plans would even leave many poor families worse off than they are under current welfare programs. Indeed, Gans has suggested that the defunct Family Assistance Plan was not the dramatic income distribution scheme that Moynihan and others billed it to be, because it would not have significantly raised incomes for most poor families, particularly those families above the lowest income level.[38]

Gottschalk has developed this critique further by questioning a basic assumption of most minimum-income plans. In particular, these plans perpetuate "the assumption that 'nonworking' persons should be consigned to live on a defined minimum income." [39] In his view such a low minimum income for those who cannot work undermines the sense of self-worth and self-respect; it separates stigmatized recipients from the rest of the community. So Gottschalk has proposed as an alternative a community-based welfare system in which recipients can become shareholders in a community-controlled organization that dispenses welfare aid in return for the performance of tasks, however small, beneficial to the community, including child rearing and caring for the aged.

Some conservative critics of guaranteed-income proposals have been concerned about the higher costs, in terms of government spending and taxes, which all programs would entail. Certainly, the costs vary from one program to the next. The additional federal government cost of Friedman's negative income tax proposal has been estimated at $2 billion, while the cost of Tobin's 1968 guaranteed-income proposal has been put at $17 billion.[40] The Theobald proposal would probably cost even more and has even been criticized by supporters of more modest income-guarantee plans. Moderate and conservative criticism of the income proposals, including Nixon's Family Assistance Plan, have often focused on the higher taxes required. One writer has estimated that an income guarantee of $2,400 would require "a 21 percent increase in the average Federal income tax rate."[41] The argument is that it is unrealistic to believe Congress will accept such increased tax rates.

As have advocates, the critics of guaranteed-income proposals have also raised the work issue.[42] "Inherent in any income guarantee scheme is the danger of disincentive."[43] Most advocates, such as Friedman, are acutely aware of this and have their minimum level of income low. Vadakin believes that the problem of work incentive is a serious one, even in the case of the more conservative proposals. The high "taxes" or discounts on the earnings of poor families provided in these plans would be a disincentive to work, particularly for those near the breakeven point.

To many critics those proposals without a strict work requirement violate ethical values held by the American people: "In the American ethic, the role of work is given a significant place as a means of personal fulfillment and satisfaction. To many, the thought that the right to income should be separated from work would be repugnant." [44] Carefully reviewing various *objections* to a guaranteed minimum income for the poor, Wogaman suggests that the following are the main lines of the moral argument among those opposing guaranteed incomes: (1) the injustice of income without work; (2) the erosion of human creativity because of the absence of a work requirement; (3) the undermining of the sense of social fulfillment; (4) the incompetence and immorality of poor people; and (5) the decrease of social control over the immoral poor.[45] These arguments, shared by members of the governing elite and average Americans, should now have a familiar ring. Although they are most relevant to plans without a work requirement, such as those of Friedman and Theobald, they have appeared in discussions of other programs involving income guarantees.

Yet other critics of guaranteed-income proposals have noted the frequent lack of concern with creation of jobs and manpower training. The intent of this critique has often been to stress the need for the federal government to create more jobs for the poor.[46] From this point of view, welfare, or other alternatives focusing on income maintenance, does not directly expand the number of meaningful jobs at decent wages: "Hence, more welfare does not mean less poverty." [47] Yet some advocates of a guaranteed income, as well as members of influential ruling elites, do not see the contradiction between work critiques of welfare and the lack of decent-paying jobs. Schiller notes that a recent survey of rural employers found them saying that jobs were readily available for welfare recipients— and that recipients were lazy—although very few (2 percent) of them reported they had any appropriate job openings.[48] In the late 1960s, influenced by images of lazy welfare recipients, part of the Congress and President Nixon pressed the work requirement in an income-guarantee package. Yet at the same time there was no serious commitment to providing the number of decent-paying jobs for many of the poor workers who would by this new plan be added to the aid rolls. Nixon proposed training 150,000 of the new aid recipients, but this was only a drop in the bucket compared to the millions of unemployed and seriously underemployed poor persons in the United States. Romanyshyn's comment was accurate: "It is extremely doubtful that a sufficient number of jobs will be created to match the skills of FAP beneficiaries either by the private sector or through government intervention, or that there will be a sufficient investment in manpower programs and supportive services to significantly enhance employment opportunities for this group." [49]

THE JOB-GUARANTEE APPROACH

This critique of guaranteed-income proposals for not providing the jobs necessary for sustaining many unemployed and underemployed poor persons has sometimes been tied to proposals for federal government intervention in employment. The strategy proposed is one of creating a large number of new jobs as a way of meeting the needs of the poor or the unemployed, even if it means coercing industry or providing large-scale public works programs. As we have seen in the 1969 and 1972 surveys analyzed earlier, there is considerable public support for such an approach. Indeed, the 1972 survey found that nearly three-quarters of the respondents supported a guaranteed-job approach if it did not entail significantly higher taxes. The support was substantially greater than for a guaranteed income. Of course, a costly program of this workfare type would find considerably less than a majority of adult Americans in support.

Thus it may seem surprising that guaranteed-income proposals which would include dual-parent families with unemployed workers have received greater leadership attention, commentary, and action in the last decade than major guaranteed-work proposals. Indeed, as far as we can determine, there have been few public advocates of extensive job-creation plans. As an alternative to Nixon's earlier welfare reform package, Schiller has suggested that a large number of decent-paying jobs must be supplied by the government to deal with the basic problems of many poor workers.[50] In his view the Family Assistance Plan would have done little about this broader problem which affects large numbers of the non-welfare poor; the same would be true of Friedman's negative income tax plan and some of the other guaranteed-income proposals. Some advocates of a guaranteed income, such as James Tobin, have emphasized the need for manpower training programs to go along with a guaranteed income; but, as in the case of Nixon's plan, little thought has been given by such advocates to job creation on a scale sufficient to meet unemployment or underemployment problems in the United States.

It is interesting that the demise of the Family Assistance Plan led to a new emphasis, up to this point in time (mid-1974) primarily rehetorical, on large numbers of jobs for the poor. By 1973 the Nixon Administration was taking economic action in areas indirectly related to job creation and was talking about stepped-up efforts to identify jobs and to put recipients to work on public jobs where private jobs are scarce. Yet the stress was on temporary and low-paying employment at public expense. This is a critical feature of the few government proposals discussed recently; there is little serious concern for the character of the jobs created, except that they be low-paying and temporary. Such proposals would likely lead to dead-end situations stigmatized as welfare jobs. Nixon's emphasis on compulsory workfare again showed a "lack of concern for the types of jobs created, their ultimate impact on poverty reduction, and the President's tendency to portray welfare recipients as being pushed kicking and screaming into the world of work." [51]

The idea of public jobs created by the federal government goes back at least to the Depression of the 1930s. For a few years in the mid-1930s the federal government was engaged in job creation with the explicit goal of reducing both poverty and revolutionary potential. Support for the federal government as the "employer of last resort" arose in the last decade. The welfare crisis, as well as persisting unemployment and growing protest, seems to have motivated many of those advocating job-guarantee plans. In the mid-1960s the National Commission on Technology, Automation and Economic Progress suggested a guaranteed-job approach. As a solution to poverty and welfare problems the federal government should become the "employer of last resort," guaranteeing jobs to those who could not find them elsewhere.[52] Those now among the unemployed should be provided with education, training, and other labor market services; and employers should be encouraged to expand the demand for products in order to provide new jobs.[53] For the unemployable the Commission recommended a guaranteed income. The proposal of the Commission was new in that the proposal was to guarantee jobs for all workers even in a period with unemployment levels considerably below the crisis levels of the 1930s.

After the National Commission report was publicized, the idea of the federal government as the "employer of last resort" spread and received serious consideration in some business and government circles. Yet Garth L. Mangum notes that "the growing advocacy might not survive if its implications were necessarily employment of over five million people at an annual budget of as much as $25 billion." [54] So Mangum suggested a more modest guaranteed-job plan, involving fewer public jobs and an additional expense of only $5 billion. Viewing manpower programs as too limited to do much about unemployment, he advocated permanent, noncompetitive employment for disabled and older workers; for other workers, he proposed a job-guarantee program with potential for advancement. One feasible public sector plan might be an entry-level employment program "to provide funds to state and local governments to pay the wages of additional employees of prescribed characteristics, to be scattered among regular public employees, perhaps without even the recipients themselves knowing of their special status." [55] This might solve the problem of stigmatized jobs. A proposal for increased subsidies to private industry to hire the unemployed is accented. More careful planning in this area is urged, but Mangum is convinced that a job-guarantee approach is a workable plan for dealing with poverty and welfare problems. Moreover, by 1967 President Lyndon Johnson had officially given his verbal support for the federal government as "employer of last resort," and the idea was finding some support among labor leaders and among other social scientists.

Some advocates of a guaranteed-job approach, such as Congressman Thomas Curtis, apparently did not mean guaranteed jobs, but rather accentuated work training and some government subsidies for the private sector.[56] In his War on Poverty, Johnson stressed similar strategies. The emphasis was on work training, education, community action, and social services rather than on restructuring the economy to provide a large number of new jobs at government expense. The goal was to fit the poor into the system rather than to involve government in job guarantees. It was one thing to support in a few words the idea of government as an "employer of last resort"; it was quite another to map out concrete action. Moderate and conservative economic writers have, on occasion, been more favorably inclined to work guarantees than to income guarantees. One writer has noted a major advantage of a job-guarantee approach: "Probably the foremost advantage of a firm work requirement backed up by guaranteed jobs is that it would make Federal aid more acceptable." [57]

Criticism of the job-guarantee approach in itself seems less widespread than criticism of guaranteed incomes, perhaps because the work emphasis ties in well with the work ethic orientations of both liberal and conservative analysts and of the general public as well. Yet a few critics of the job approach have pointed up the problems of all labor-centered measures. We have already noted the critique of schemes emphasizing temporary and low-paying jobs. Moreover, "creating jobs, training people for jobs, retraining people for different jobs—all of these miss the mark." [58] The idea of these critics is that jobs do not provide secure incomes over the long term. Theobald's analysis of automation and the future supports this perspective. Arguing in a more radical way, Kelso and Hetler suggest that workers must also be given access to the factor responsible for recent economic growth and for productivity—*capital*. The threat of obsolescence faces every worker. The only answer to this is control of capital. "It is the institutions of society, not parental genes, that bestow the blessings of ownership of productive capital." [59] Wealth is the result of the ownership or control of such things as real estate and shares of stock. In the view of Kelso and Hetler an adequate aid program would provide the propertyless with access to property and newly formed capital.

MORE ECONOMIC EQUALITY: RADICAL REDISTRIBUTION

The 1969 survey question on equalizing incomes for families drew heavy opposition from those in all income groups, not just the most affluent. No less than 80 percent of the sample opposed relatively equal income for families. So it is not surprising that in recent years there have been very few advocates of real economic equality, or even substantial redistribution of income, as a way of solving welfare and poverty problems.

In the American past there have been a few notable advocates of greatly increased economic equality, including such men as Henry George, Upton Sinclair, Francis E. Townsend, and Huey Long. In the late nineteenth century Henry George wrote a famous book, *Progress and Poverty*, which advocated the abolition of the monopoly of land by the few. This was to be done by shifting taxes from labor to land—one single tax on the value of land. George was sanguine about the major distributive effects of his radical plan, for the single land tax "would secure justice in distribution." [60] Although various socialist groups in the decades between *Progress and Poverty* and the 1930s advised major economic reform, perhaps the most widely known advocates of more equality emerged in the 1930s. At that time, Upton Sinclair started a movement oriented to substantial income redistribution; the movement advocated "stiffer income and inheritance taxes, a tax on idle land, a fifty-dollar monthly pension to needy persons over sixty, and a huge network of cooperatives to stimulate production, consumption and employment." [61] Perhaps the most famous advocate of "sharing the wealth" in the 1930s was Senator Huey Long of Louisiana. Long proposed a plan for wealth redistribution so that every "deserving family" might have a truly adequate income. [62]

More recently, few analysts have explicitly set forth a program for substantial income redistribution from the wealthy to those below. John Rawls, a socially oriented philosopher, has argued for new ethical principles linked to greater equality. In his view a just and well-ordered society requires equal liberty, opportunity, and wealth. [63] Rawls argues that inequality, which is only to be permitted in his ideal society if it benefits the entire community, will not be excessive and will in fact be considerably less than what has traditionally prevailed in human societies. Although these ethical principles are not spelled out in terms of a concrete income distribution program, they could provide the framework for a society with substantially less economic inequality.

Herbert Gans is one of the few recent authors to publicly propose radical economic redistribution beyond that envisaged by most advocates of a guaranteed minimum income.[64] Yet even Gans rejects collectivist approaches to a more egalitarian America for an approach that will maintain private property and much of the basic structure of the existing economic system. In his strategy for more equality he would press for distributing stock ownership to ordinary workers. A major extension of social services, such as medical services, would also be a good first step. However, an income strategy would maximize free choice. "Unemployment and under-employment have to be eliminated, and the poverty line raised so that the gaps between those at the bottom, middle, and top are reduced and no one earns less than 60 percent of the median income and eventually no less than 70 percent: $7,000 for a family of four by today's census figures and income definition."[65] This 60–70 percent of median income figure is a level well above that suggested in most guaranteed-income proposals.

Gans would apparently require that those able to work do so. In his view a comprehensive distribution scheme encompassing the poor could also subsidize private industry in order to expand jobs and could require the federal government to be the "employer of last resort."[66] Thus in his analysis Gans combines elements of guaranteed-income and guaranteed-job plans, together with the additional redistributive idea of substantial tax reform. Perhaps most important, he is one of few analysts to suggest the need for some type of *ceiling on incomes,* although he is vague as to the exact placement of this ceiling.

In a concluding chapter of his book *More Equality,* Gans lays out an even more radical economic equality scenario, a speculative model for the future, which assumes "the retention of wage differentials, with equality achieved annually or more often through the tax system, enabling all adult individuals to have equal incomes, with cost-level allowances for children determined both by their number and age."[67] As a result, serious poverty and great affluence would disappear, and average incomes for four-person families would probably be in the $15,000 to $20,000 range. Obviously, such income redistribution would require a major downward shift of income from the very affluent and would have profound social effects on everything from housing construction to work incentives. Doubtless, symbolic rewards would have to replace money as a work incentive. Gans admits this is a utopian model and apparently does not advocate it for the near future; nonetheless, it is important, he argues, to think out the implications of such speculative models in order to understand the implications of more modest proposals for income redistribution.

Of course, there are few prominent critics who have dealt specifically with radical egalitarianism of this type, primarily because there have been so few advocates of major income or wealth redistribution. Yet we have seen previously how the fear of material equality, or equal economic outcomes, paralyzes conservative economists such as Milton Friedman. His negative income tax plan is specifically and carefully distinguished from egalitarian schemes. And we have seen Daniel P. Moynihan's critique of those who would advocate class equality. Clearly, a proposal for "privilege for all"—or even one moving substantially toward that goal—strikes fear into the hearts of most Americans, whether they are members of the governing elites or average citizens. Proposals for moving toward equality of wealth, or income, or power have so far not been accorded a serious hearing.

CONCLUSION

The 1969 and 1972 survey data, as well as other materials we have examined in this book, suggest that the work-oriented ideology of individualism persists in the United States and has had a shaping effect, direct and indirect, on private and public approaches to dealing with poor persons. Although contemporary Americans may be more willing than earlier Americans to accept some government action on behalf of the poor, there seem to be clear limitations on acceptable strategies. As long as the majority individualize or personalize social problems to a substantial degree, viewing problems in terms of immoral or character-defective individuals, attempts at significant redistributive or structural reform will probably be extraordinarily difficult. Individualistic interpretations mesh well with attempts to maintain the existing status quo, or to tinker with it only a little, whereas structural interpretations lend themselves to major attempts at substantial reform of the society.

Individualism, as measured in the 1969 nationwide survey, was found to relate strongly to negativism toward traditional welfare programs and alternative poor relief approaches. Indeed, only a minority of those interviewed supported the three innovative proposals we used in the surveys, with the exception of a guaranteed-job program involving no significant increase in taxes. This was true in both the 1969 and 1972 surveys. Such data support Wilensky's argument that one of the reasons the United States has been a "reluctant welfare state," compared to a number of European countries, has been the strength of the broad ideology of individualism.[68] The ideology of individualism seems to be a persisting constraint on the development and implementation of new public policies for aiding the poor. The relationship of American views of the poor and government action toward the poor is an intimate and reciprocal one going back for several centuries. Indeed, it is difficult to separate the two.

The reluctance of major socioreligious groups to support substantial income redistribution or major job-creation programs is clearly seen in the survey data. It is among white Protestants and white Catholics that one finds the least support for major alterations in the present economic structure. This can be seen as a sign of false consciousness, because many low- and middle-income workers in these groups might benefit greatly from major redistributive programs. Such views tend to depoliticize the country, in that the attention of workers is focused on the government benefits the poor would receive rather than on benefits to middle-income Americans. Here the ideology of competitive individualism, ingrained into Americans at all class levels, is intimately tied in with the economic structure of Western capitalism and has been propagated by that structure for centuries. The same is also true of related belief systems focused on private property and free enterprise. Support has been won for the capitalist system and its structure of inequality through schools, churches, the media, industry, and government.

Of course, the ideology of individualism is not the only important constraint on significant departures in public policy toward poverty and welfare. Members of the elite groups—particularly those in education, business, and government—usually determine what specifically happens in regard to public policy. Modest alternatives to welfare, such as existing guaranteed-income and guaranteed-job proposals, were supported first by some in the academic elite, then by some in the business elite, and later, if at all, by important government officials. Often, it seems that some members of dominant elite groups were seriously considering modest redistributive proposals that most of the public would not accept. Why has this occurred? This intriguing question can perhaps be answered in terms of elite fears about rising welfare costs, about low-wage work, and about the revolutionary potential of minority workers. Some members seemed to be searching for a new income-maintenance mechanism that would help resolve the "welfare crisis" and the "revolution of rising expectations." Some have been willing to make modest redistributive sacrifices in order to retain the basic structure of inequality, while others have resisted all such attempts, however modest they might be. Indeed, we have not yet seen the implementation of modest proposals.

Because these people with power have the most to lose from threats to the basic institutions of capitalism, it is not surprising that a few are among the first to consider seriously new departures in public policy in troubled times. Yet the ideology of individualism seems to have set limits even for these elite-generated policy proposals, both in the past and in the present. Innovations within the welfare system itself, as well as new departures ranging from the War on Poverty to Nixon's Family Assistance Plan, have been pervaded by concerns for the work ethic and the maintenance of the institutions of capitalism. It has been difficult to generate widespread elite support for such departures. Innovations in poverty policy, moreover, have not meant an abdication of the work ethic. The War on Poverty, for example, can be viewed as an attempt to meet poverty problems that focused heavily on employment-related or educational services and on integrating the unemployed poor into the economy. The payoff for capitalism, however, may have been greater than for the poor. Some defusing of revolutionary action perhaps occurred, and "training subsidies were direct subsidies to the very corporate interest whose power has thwarted the abolition of poverty in America." [69] The point is that even modest new departures in poverty policy are usually in line with, or shaped to fit, the economic interests of dominant elites, with the downward redistributive impact kept to a reasonable minimum.

The one actual attempt to get a very modest guaranteed minimum income plan beyond the discussion stage occurred in the late 1960s, when President Nixon proposed a Family Assistance Plan. This program, a significant but not revolutionary reshaping of the existing welfare system, was also pervaded by the ideology of individualism and the other concerns of the ruling elite. FAP was seen as a way of replacing the current crisis-ridden welfare system with something more work-oriented; it also aimed at alleviating the fiscal crises of state and local governments. Concern for the suffering of the poor themselves, however, had second priority in that proposal, which was eventually defeated. More recently, trial balloons have appeared in the press indicating a concern among some in the new Gerald Ford Administration to revive the family assistance proposal. Whether or not the mid-1970s will see the implementation of this type of modest redistributive scheme yet remains to be seen. Significantly, such a plan would necessitate a further federalization of the American welfare system.

Nonetheless, little serious attention has been given in recent years to *major* income or wealth redistribution in this society. It is in the interests of those with power and wealth to preserve the structure of inequality basically as it is. In addition, opposition to an equality revolution, Gans has suggested, may come from a new "conservatism" emergent in the United States, in part fostered by the governing elite and in part a response to an exaggerated view of the gains of the poor and of black Americans in recent years.[70] Yet this is not really a new conservatism; the ideology of individualism has maintained inequality throughout American history.

POSTSCRIPT

One final question remains for those concerned about a significant departure in public policy in the direction of substantially greater equality in opportunity, wealth, and power in the United States. The question is how to change the system in the direction of more equality. In responding to this, some may emphasize changing ideologies, while others may stress protest organization among class-conscious workers and other dissidents.

Just possibly, a slow shift may be underway toward greater emphasis among average Americans on the more impersonal social and economic forces as they affect social problems, including poverty—and perhaps toward greater support for structure-oriented reform programs. A significant proportion of the respondents in the 1969 survey placed some emphasis on the role of the more impersonal social and economic factors in determining poverty, either taken alone or in conjunction with individualistic and fatalistic factors. The under-30 respondents were less likely than the over-50 generation to place heavy emphasis on individualistic factors; they were also somewhat more likely to rank high on the structural-factors index.[71] Whether or not this will continue as they become older remains to be seen.

Important too in any assessments of ideological change are certain racial and ethnic groups. It is among those most committed to the structural approach, blacks and other minorities, that we find the greatest support for major economic reform such as guaranteed incomes and guaranteed jobs. Yet, because white Protestants and Catholics comprise the political majority, the policy views of black Americans and others in a similar subordinate position probably will prevail only with great difficulty, although their influence may now be on the rise.

Yet another sign of change may be the slowly growing amount of research questioning conventional beliefs. Though we have not here systematically dealt with the adequacy or accuracy of all the beliefs in the work-oriented ideology of individualism—that is a task for a book in itself—it is important to note that a number of recent research studies have seriously questioned fundamental American attitudes about work and success. Recent studies have found no significant differences between the work attitudes of different classes of Americans. Anderson notes that most workers would continue to work even if they could have a modest income without work. Most people rely on work for their sense of self-worth and for social acceptance.

In response to the question "If by some chance you had enough money to live comfortably without working, do you think that you would work anyway, or would you not work?" over four fifths of a sample of blue-collar men studied by Tausky reported that they *would work anyway*.[72]

The same has been found to be true of white-collar and, most important, even for chronically unemployed workers. And, as we have noted previously, a number of studies have shown a strong work ethic among the poor, including the welfare poor. As yet, the New Jersey and Pennsylvania income maintenance experiments have found among the poor families studied no evidence of a massive withdrawal from work or sharp decreases in family income as the result of the income supplements and guarantees provided.[73] Other studies have suggested that there may well be few significant attitudinal differences between more and less successful Americans and that the traditional view of educational opportunity and attainment as a major road to mobility has been greatly exaggerated.[74] Conceivably, in the future this type of research may have some impact on prevailing attitudes. Ideally, attitudinal or value shifts among Americans should be examined at ten-year periods, just as we catalogue demographic characteristics in a national population census each decade. All in all, however, there does appear to be a basis for limited optimism about the future pace of change toward greater recognition of fundamental structural flaws.

On the one hand, it may be that truly major alterations in America's institutionalized approach to welfare and poverty, necessitating as they would large-scale changes in existing economic arrangements, must await a shift in basic beliefs and values toward increased structuralism and emphasis on collective and class interests. That there may be some chance for this is suggested by the materials we have just reviewed. So far, however, the typical American's orientation has been reluctant and conservative. Most working persons seem conservative ideologically, emphasizing the role of the individual both in economics and in politics. Occasional, and modest, changes in the direction of the "welfare state" seem to be accepted as a *practical* matter, often in crisis situations such as the Depression or as part of the organization of middle-income workers, but have usually not been viewed in broader ideological terms.

On the other hand, fundamental economic and political changes benefiting the poor may come primarily as the result of increased organization and militancy among those workers who are becoming or are already high in class or group awareness, as we have seen in the last decade in civil rights organizations, welfare rights activity, and unions among poor workers. Protest movements of this type have seen some limited successes, have dramatically called for thoroughgoing economic justice, and have stressed structural interpretations of social problems and the collective goal of redistributing wealth and power. Yet future victories in the equality struggle seem intimately linked to increasing the class awareness of those caught in between the wealthy and the poor, the so-called Middle Americans. Clearly, the prospects for an equality revolution of major proportions at this point are not very good, because both the "have-a-lots" and the "have-somes" would fight hard to keep their disproportionate share of wealth and power vis-à-vis the "have-nots." [75]

Convincing the "have-a-lots" that accelerated and recurrent conflict over the long run may well be the only alternative to more equality meted out in some fashion seems to be the requisite challenge for radical reformers. Perhaps more important, convincing the "have-somes" that major redistributive reform is in their interest is a major challenge. Even many among the "have-nots" are not yet inclined to major redistributive proposals. Doubtless, the ultimate prospects for an equality revolution depend on such factors as the basic health of the economy, the willingness of the governing elite to permit greater redistribution, and the amount of pressure coming from protest groups at the lower levels. Commitment to substantial economic equality has never been very great in the United States; at best, we have seen policies involving relatively modest cost and modest redistribution, at least to those at the lower economic levels. Writing in the early 1970s, we see a governmental retreat from the idea of even modest income redistribution downward. Whether the retreat can be reversed yet remains to be seen.

1. I am indebted to the Opinion Research Corporation (Princeton, N.J.) for permission to use its data from the 1972 survey. The data have been taken from Opinion Research Corporation, *Public Opinion Index*, 30 (May 1972), 1–8. For the source of the 1969 data, see the asterisked footnote at the beginning of the previous

chapter. Some of the "alternative" questions were patterned after similar questions used by the Gallup polling organization (by permission).

2. Marth N. Ozawa, "Social Welfare: the Minority Share," *Social Work*, 17 (May 1972), 37.

3. James C. Vadakin, *Children, Poverty, and Family Allowances* (New York: Basic Books, 1968), pp. 141–42; Milton Friedman, *Capitalism and Freedom* (Chicago: University of Chicago Press, 1962), pp. 191 ff.

4. Friedman, *Capitalism and Freedom*, p. 192.

5. *Ibid.*, pp. 195–200.

6. Robert Theobald, *Free Men and Free Markets* (New York: Clarkson N. Potter, Inc., 1963), pp. 141–84.

7. Robert Theobald, "Introduction," in *The Guaranteed Income*, ed. Robert Theobald (Garden City, N.Y.: Doubleday Anchor Books, 1967), p. 17.

8. Theobald, *Free Men and Free Markets*, pp. 192–95.

9. Theobald, "Introduction," p. 18.

10. *Ibid.*, pp. 18–23.

11. These two plans are summarized in David M. Gordon, "Alternative Income Maintenance Proposals," in *Problems in Political Economy*, ed. David M. Gordon (Lexington, Mass.: D. C. Heath, 1971), pp. 253–54; see also James Tobin, "Raising the Incomes of the Poor," in *Agenda for the Nation*, ed. Kermit Gordon (Washington, D.C.: The Brookings Institution, 1968), pp. 111 ff.

12. Vadakin, *Children, Poverty, and Family Allowances*, p. 146.

13. Tobin, "Raising the Incomes of the Poor," p. 113.

14. *Ibid.*, p. 115.

15. Gilbert Y. Steiner, *The State of Welfare* (Washington, D.C.: The Brookings Institution, 1971), pp. 95–96.

16. Philip Wogaman, *Guaranteed Annual Income* (Nashville, Tenn.: Abingdon Press, 1968), pp. 13–15.

17. Steiner, *The State of Welfare*, pp. 100–101.

18. *Report from the Steering Committee of the Arden House Conference on Public Welfare* (Albany, N.Y., 1968), p. 12.

19. Steiner, *The State of Welfare*, p. 103.

20. *Ibid.*, p. 105.

21. *Ibid.*, pp. 96, 117–18.

22. Daniel P. Moynihan, *The Politics of a Guaranteed Income* (New York: Vintage Books, 1973), pp. 129–30.

23. Steiner, *The State of Welfare*, pp. 110–11.

24. Moynihan, *The Politics of a Guaranteed Income*, pp. 131–82.

25. *Ibid.*, p. 173.

26. Richard M. Nixon, "Welfare Reform: A Message from the President of the United States," quoted in *Poverty Policy*, ed. Theodore R. Marmor (Chicago: Aldine, 1971), p. 77.

27. *Ibid.*, p. 78. Italics are in the original.

28. *Ibid.*, p. 78.

29. *Ibid.*, p. 83.

30. Moynihan, *The Politics of a Guaranteed Income*, p. 223. Exceptions to this would include (1) those unable to work and (2) mothers of preschool children.

31. Robert H. Finch, "Explanation of the Bill," in *Poverty Policy*, ed. Theodore R. Marmor (Chicago: Aldine, 1971), pp. 88–94.

32. Moynihan, *The Politics of a Guaranteed Income*, pp. 271–94.

33. *Ibid.*, p. 270.

34. *Ibid.*, p. 441.

35. *Ibid.*, p. 545.

36. *Ibid.*, p. 445.

37. Vadakin, *Children, Poverty, and Family Allowances*, p. 152. As an alternative to income maintenance plans, Vadakin has proposed a universal program of family allowances which would not tie income to employment. This would be financed out of federal tax revenues. Payments would be at the rate of $10 per month for each child under 18 years, with all families eligible. (*Ibid.*, p. 185.)

38. Herbert J. Gans, *More Equality* (New York: Random House, 1973), p. xiv.

39. Shimon Gottschalk, "The Community-Based Welfare System: An Alternative to Public Welfare," *The Journal of Applied Behavioral Science*, 9 (1973), 235.

40. Gordon, "Alternative Income Maintenance Proposals," p. 253.

41. Paul S. Anderson, "Pros, Cons and Some Alternatives," *New England Economic Review* (January/February 1971), p. 40.

42. *Ibid.*, pp. 41–45.

43. Vadakin, *Children, Poverty, and Family Allowances*, p. 153.

44. *Ibid.*, p. 162.

45. Wogaman, *Guaranteed Annual Income*, pp. 43–49.

46. For a discussion of automation and job creation see Charles H. Anderson, *Toward a New Sociology*, rev. ed. (Homewood, Ill.: Dorsey Press, 1974), pp. 229–33.

47. Bradley R. Schiller, "Moving from Welfare to Workfare," *Public Policy*, 21 (Winter 1973), 126. Schiller notes also that neither child-care services nor manpower training expand employment opportunities.

48. *Ibid.*, p. 127.

49. John M. Romanyshyn, *Social Welfare* (New York: Random House, 1971), p. 264.

50. Schiller, "Moving from Welfare to Workfare," p. 131.

51. *Ibid.*, p. 133.

52. National Commission on Technology, Automation and Economic Progress, *Technology and the American Economy* (Washington, D.C.: U.S. Government Printing Office, 1966).

53. See the summary and analysis in Garth L. Mangum, "Guaranteeing Employment Opportunities," in *Social Policies for America in the Seventies*, ed. Robert Theobald (Garden City, N.Y.: Doubleday, 1968), pp. 25–31.

54. *Ibid.*, p. 39.

55. *Ibid.*, p. 50.

56. Wogaman, *Guaranteed Annual Income*, p. 34.

57. Paul S. Anderson, "Pros, Cons and Some Alternatives," 44.

58. Louis O. Kelso and Patricia Hetler, "Equality of Economic Opportunity through Capital Ownership," in *Social Policies for America in the Seventies*, p. 143.

59. *Ibid.*, p. 145.

60. Henry George, *Progress and Poverty* (New York: Robert Schalkenbach Foundation, 1962), p. xv.

61. Dixon Wechter, *The Age of the Great Depression* (Chicago: Quadrangle Books, 1971), pp. 202–3.

62. *Ibid.*, pp. 205–6.

63. John Rawls, *A Theory of Justice* (Cambridge, Mass.: Harvard University Press, 1971), pp. 3–67.

64. Gans, *More Equality*.

65. *Ibid.*, p. 29.

66. *Ibid.*, p. 158.

67. *Ibid.*, p. 197.

68. Harold L. Wilensky and Charles N. Lebeaux, *Industrial Society and Social Welfare* (New York: Free Press, 1965).

69. Howard M. Wachtel, "Looking at Poverty from a Radical Perspective," in *Modern Political Economy*, ed. James H. Weaver (Boston: Allyn and Bacon, Inc., 1973), p. 221.

70. Gans, *More Equality*, pp. 29–31.

71. Although such data are generally not available for earlier decades, we do have one roughly comparable survey question, asked nearly 25 years before the 1969 survey. In 1945 the Office of Public Opinion Research at Princeton conducted a survey with one question asking for explanations "why some of the people are always poor." The results revealed very heavy emphasis on individualistic interpretations, such as lack of effort and initiative, individual mismanagement, poor character, and similar responses. Relatively few respondents cited societal factors such as the lack of job and educational opportunities, low wages, or exploitation by the rest of the society. Although the coding was different in the two surveys, the data suggest the speculation that there has been somewhat of a shift since 1945 in the direction of greater emphasis on the inadequacies of the existing system. See Richard Centers, "Attitudes and Belief in Relation to Occupational Stratification," *Journal of Social Psychology*, 27 (1948), 159–85.

72. Anderson, *Toward a New Sociology*, p. 232.

73. Joseph Heffernan, "Negative Income Tax Studies," *Social Service Review*, 46 (March 1972), 12.

74. Christopher Jencks et al., *Inequality* (New York: Basic Books, 1972).

75. My thinking on these matters has been influenced by Gans's book, *More Equality*.

Index